INCREASE YOUR WEALTH AND INVEST IN THE BEAR MARKET

THE BEST RECESSION PROOF STRATEGIES

© Copyright Publications 2020 - All rights reserved.

The content contained within this book may not be reproduced, duplicated or transmitted without direct written permission from the author or the publisher.

Under no circumstances will any blame or legal responsibility be held against the publisher, or author, for any damages, reparation, or monetary loss due to the information contained within this book, either directly or indirectly.

Legal Notice:

This book is copyright protected. It is only for personal use. You cannot amend, distribute, sell, use, quote or paraphrase any part, or the content within this book, without the consent of the author or publisher.

Disclaimer Notice:

The following work is presented for informational purposes only. None of the information herein constitutes an offer to sell or buy any security or investment vehicle, nor does it constitute an investment recommendation of a legal, tax, accounting or investment recommendation by Freeman Publications, its employees or paid contributors. The information is presented without regard for individual investment preferences or risk parameters and is general, non-tailored, non-specific information.

Freeman Publications, including all employees and paid contributors, agree not to trade in any security they write about for a minimum of three days (72 hours) following publication of a new article, book, report or email. Except for existing orders that were in place before submission (any such orders will also always be disclosed inside the document). This includes equity, options, debt, or other instruments directly related to that security, stock, or company. The author may have indirect positions in some companies mentioned due to holdings in mutual funds, ETFs, Closed End Funds or other similar vehicles, and there is no guarantee that the author is aware of the individual portfolios of any of those funds at any given time. Such indirect holdings will generally not be disclosed.

Warning: There is no magic formula to getting rich, in the financial markets or otherwise. Investing often involves high risks and you can lose a lot of money. Success in investment vehicles with the best prospects for price appreciation can only be achieved through proper and rigorous research and analysis. Please do not invest with money you cannot afford to lose. The opinions in this content are just that, opinions of the authors. We are a publishing company and the opinions, comments, stories, reports, advertisements and articles we publish are for informational and educational purposes only; nothing herein should be considered personalized investment advice. Before you make any investment, check with your investment professional (advisor). We urge our readers to review the financial statements and prospectus of any company they are interested in. We are not responsible for any damages or losses arising from the use of any information herein. Past performance is not a guarantee of future results.

This work is based on SEC filings, current events, interviews, corporate press releases, and what we've learned as financial journalists. It may contain errors and you shouldn't make any investment decision based solely on what you read here. It is your money and your responsibility.

Freeman Publications Ltd. are 100% independent in that we are not affiliated with any security, investment vehicle, bank or brokerage house.

CONTENTS

Your Worst Nightmare, or the Greatest Opportunity of the Decade?

1. Without a Bubble, There Is No Crash—A Practical Look at Economic Cycles
2. Bear Market Timelines and Emotional Management
3. The Onion - Adopting the Rational Process Investing Model for a Bear Market
4. Navigating the Flaws in Human Psychology
5. How To Capitalize Effectively in a Bear Market
6. How to Hedge Your Current Portfolio
7. Protecting Your Portfolio & Generating Extra Monthly Income With Risk-Averse Options Strategies
8. How To Prepare for the Absolute Worst
9. Preparing for the Next Time—What To Do at the End of a Bull Market
10. How To Identify Fraudulent Operations

References

"WE CONTINUE TO EXPECT THAT MARKETS (AND OUR PERFORMANCE) WILL REMAIN VOLATILE, AND THEREFORE, NEW OPPORTUNITIES MAY PRESENT THEMSELVES THAT ARE SUPERIOR TO INVESTMENTS WE CURRENTLY OWN."

YOUR WORST NIGHTMARE, OR THE GREATEST OPPORTUNITY OF THE DECADE?

Bear markets are perhaps the average investor's worst nightmare. After all, why would anyone ever want them? These are times of maximum pessimism. Everything financial instrument seems to be going down and entire economies appear close to collapse. The mainstream financial news usually confirms this point of view.

Wall Street slaps the entire market with one big "SELL" rating and if you log in to your brokerage account, all you see is red everywhere. Tough times indeed.

Making money in a bull market is quite straightforward. A rising tide lifts all boats! When bullish sentiment pervades the market, it looks as if every company's stock rises and investment is a straightforward endeavor. Why does every company's stock rise? This is because in the short term, sentiment is what drives market prices, not fundamentals.

This same sentiment is what makes investing in a bear market so difficult. All of us carry within us a psychological bias called the herd mentality. If you see a large number of people turning their heads to the left, you'll turn left to see what's going on as well. This is an automatic reaction that is deeply connected to our survival mechanism.

Similarly, if you see people selling everything in the market, you'll want to follow suit. It takes a huge amount of awareness and conviction to go against the tide. However, this is where big money is made.

For example, the investor Sir John Templeton made a fortune in the bear markets that preceded World War II (Chen, 2019). Once war was declared, the market slumped thanks to doomsday expectations. Templeton borrowed money and bought 100 shares each in 104 companies that were selling for less than a dollar in the American markets. As a historical refresher, Europe was being subjected to the Blitzkrieg at this point and it seemed as if Hitler's armies would overrun Western Europe entirely (which they did.)

This is when Templeton not only bought shares in companies but borrowed money to finance his purchases! Over the next five years, his portfolio grew by more than 400% and he made a fortune for himself.

This just goes to show that bear markets offer smart investors immense opportunities. The key word to recognize here is "smart."

SMART MONEY VS. DUMB MONEY

The notion of smart versus dumb money has always been present in the markets. The typical line on this is that institutional investors are the smart money while the average retail investor represents dumb money.

This isn't true at all. If institutional investors are uniformly smart, how can one explain the variety of financial crises that have occurred? If they were all smart, Bear Stearns and Lehman Brothers would still be around, not to mention the large number of hedge funds that have sunk without a trace. The real distinction between dumb and smart money lies in the process that each group follows.

Smart investors always have a process that they follow. Their processes are based on rigorous and intelligent principles of investing. Dumb money, on the other hand, has either no process or their process usually boils down to jumping into stocks that are in the news.

Developing an investment process is not a simple thing. You can read all the quotes and listen to all the interviews of famous investors such as Warren Buffett, Charlie Munger or Benjamin Graham, but mere reading isn't going to help you. You still need to work at reigning in your emotions to avoid plunging into some hot stock just because it jumped 12% in a single day.

Helping you develop a rational investing process is what this book aims to do. On the surface, this may seem like a tough task. A study conducted by Bernstein Advisors found that the average active investor realizes just 2.1% per year in gains (Bernstein, 2018). That's less than U.S. Treasury bills! A Treasury bill is a bond that is issued by the American government with a maturity date of less than one year. T-bills, as they're called, are viewed as a safe investment and contain as little risk for the investor as possible. In short, all the investor needs to do is place their money in T-bills and forget about them.

The only asset class that returned less than the average investor over the past 20 years is Japanese equities. So if all that activity in the market produces a return on par with T-bills, is investing even worth it? The answer to this question lies in the study itself.

Bernstein Advisors determined that the abysmal rate of return was caused by investors' timing of asset allocation decisions. Simply put, they bought assets that were overvalued and sold ones that were undervalued. It's easy to understand why this happens.

Many new investors enter the market with the hope of making quick and easy money. They jump into a hot stock that has been promoted in the financial media and hope to see the price rise. They keep checking in every day to monitor the stock price, as if they could influence its movement!

However, that heavily promoted stock has seen millions of people enter at the same time, for similar reasons as the investor in question. In short, the price is inflated well above what it's truly worth. What happens to assets that are overvalued? Simple. Their price corrects back to what it's truly worth.

The result is a decline in price and panic for the investor. The stock is no longer in the news and no one seems to be talking about it. Investors rationalize that they must have been wrong and sell their investments. The millions of other investors who entered for the same reason are doing the exact same thing at this point.

The huge selling pressure results in the stock's price dipping below what it's truly worth. In short, all of these investors sell right when the stock is a bargain. This is how a 2.1% return is made in the markets.

The Social Media Cycle

These days the news cycle is 24/7. Social media is constantly on and the excessive amount of information that is available these days is a double-edged sword. On one hand, you can access a large amount of credible research on obscure companies. On the other hand, too much information can cause you to miss the forest for the trees.

Social media also makes it easy for you to jump in and out of stocks. Company CEOs are present on Twitter these days and anything that they say can upset stock prices. Elon Musk and Tesla are a good example of this. Information is valuable only if you align it with an intelligent process.

Without this, all that information turns against you because you begin to rely on your emotional processes to make decisions. Our objective in writing this book is to help you develop rational processes that will help you filter this information. You'll learn what to pay attention to and what to ignore.

Most importantly, we're not going to focus on things such as market timing or active trading methods. These are not intelligent methods of investing. Instead, if you wish to make money over the long term, you're going to have to develop a strong process for yourself and this is what we're going to show you.

Along the way, we'll also help you eliminate the perception that a bear market is a bad thing. There is no need for you to renounce the US dollar and stockpile supplies or ammo just because the market scenario looks bad. In fact, this is a great time to be investing in the market. This isn't some emotional proclamation we're making, it's grounded in fact, as you'll learn.

You'll discover about a few alternative investments that work brilliantly in bear markets. We'll be discussing gold, as well as cryptocurrencies. These asset classes have been pushed as hedges against the dollar. However, going all-in on these is not an intelligent move. You'll learn exactly what sort of an approach you need to adopt when it comes to such alternative investments.

Above all else, we're pragmatists. Our short-term outlook for the world's economy is less than positive. However, this is not a doomsday book. The long-term view is what matters above all else when it comes to investing, and our view for the global economy is extremely positive.

We might be long-term bulls, but this doesn't mean we cannot take short-term practicalities into consideration. Managing both sides of the equation intelligently is what you're going to learn.

Now that you know what to expect in this book, let's jump in and look at market cycles and what they mean for your investment process.

1
WITHOUT A BUBBLE, THERE IS NO CRASH—A PRACTICAL LOOK AT ECONOMIC CYCLES

Crashes don't occur without assets being overvalued. After all, something that is selling for what it's truly worth is unlikely to see a large price correction. Bubbles are what cause crashes and ever since economies have existed, the markets have witnessed cycles of bubbles and crashes.

The frequency of such events has not been fixed over the years. However, all economic cycles move through certain stages. All of these stages have telltale signs that you can spot in advance. Understanding the mechanics of these stages will help you figure out which part of the boom/bust cycle we're in currently and tailor your investments accordingly.

STAGE ONE: IT ALL STARTS WITH DISRUPTION

Every bubble starts off with a seed of justification. What we mean is that it has a foundation in reality. More often than not, a new process or paradigm makes itself known in the markets and this changes the way things are done. Disruption by itself is not a bad thing.

For example, the past decade has witnessed huge levels of disruption that we're still coming to terms with. Internet companies have existed since the turn of the millennium and going back to the mid 90s. However, comparing the technology and the way in which we communicate these days makes the early 2000s seem like the Middle Ages.

Consider the fact that Facebook and smartphones didn't exist back then and you'll see the level to which our world has changed. Amazon was a bookseller and Google was smaller than Yahoo Search. Disruptions of these kinds cause changes that take time for us to process.

Much like a child learning a new skill, we navigate this new world through trial and error as we feel our way forward. Technology companies have cornered the market when it comes to the word disruption, but the phenomenon has been occurring for a long time now.

For example, the fall of the Soviet Union was an example of an event that disrupted the world's economy. China's decision to open its economy in the late 1970s was another decision that took some time to make an impact. Looking at how strong China is these days, no one will argue against the fact that this was a seminal decision in history.

Disruption comes in two forms. It either occurs through technological advancement or through some fundamental economic change. Often one ties into the other.

Technological Advancement

Technology has always played a huge role in human advancement. You might think we're referring to the dotcom boom or the digital revolution, but our example is more ancient than that. The first huge leap forward that Western economies witnessed occurred in the 1760s.

It's tough to pinpoint the exact moment when it all began, but the invention of the steam engine is usually thought of as the event that sparked change. James Watt managed to greatly improve existing steam engine designs in 1759, and soon wind and labor-powered machines were replaced by steam engines. Suddenly, railroads were a thing!

This in turn led to the creation of factories and other machinery that changed the rate at which countries could produce goods. It also created a huge gap between the haves and the have-nots in the world, and soon imperialism was in full swing thanks to the need for raw materials.

The Industrial Revolution created an advantage for Western economies to such an extent that the world order is still based on the prosperity it produced. While the exact nature of that order has changed, there's no denying that the technological advances witnessed during this period have sustained those economies for a long time now.

The dotcom boom is another example of technological disruption changing the way we look at business. While this is mostly associated with the dotcom crash in 2000, it doesn't change the fact that the explosion of internet-based companies shifted our perception of business and value.

Companies such as Amazon and eBay were born in the mid 90s. Sergey Brin and Larry Page would not have devoted much time to creating a search algorithm if the internet didn't open possibilities to retrieve information. Elon Musk would not have had the money to buy Tesla if he hadn't created PayPal in the 90s along with Peter Thiel.

Over the past decade, the development of the Software as a Service (SaaS) business model has disrupted revenue collection models. A SaaS model asks the consumer to pay a monthly fee for accessing the software instead of having them pay once for purchasing it.

In the early 2000s, you could buy McAfee's antivirus, or Adobe's Photoshop software with a one-time payment. Which would then grant you lifetime access to it. These days, you pay these companies a monthly fee for usage and get access to automatic updates. This represents a smaller upfront payment to the consumer, and increased lifetime revenues for the provider. The SaaS model has moved into brick and mortar industries too. Tesla has brought some elements of the SaaS model to the automobile market with its cars receiving software updates via the cloud.

Fundamental Economic Change

The other major source of disruption is when fundamental economic disruptions occur. Communism versus capitalism was the heavyweight bout that gripped the world from the second World War till 1990. Everything in the world revolved around what America and the USSR were involved in.

Wars were started, space was explored, man stepped on the moon and countries' entire economies were dictated by which brand of politics they preferred. Thus, in 1989 when the USSR fell, no one was quite sure of how things would play out. The opening up of Russia's economy provided massive opportunity to a certain group of people.

For the first time in a long time, Eastern European countries had to stop worrying about a big brother being present and govern themselves. It was a monumental shock to the world's system, in other words.

Lending standards have always been a reliable indicator of fundamental economic changes taking place. The invention of mass consumer lending in the 1920s and the relaxation of credit standards in the early to mid 2000s are examples of financial changes that disrupted the way economies ran.

The disruption stage is characterized by optimism and opportunity. This is when things are beginning to boom and investors are beginning to take notice. They typically begin moving capital into these economies or opportunities.

STAGE TWO: THE BULL MARKET

Once more and more people begin to recognize the disruption, the amount of money that is piled into these opportunities increases. The result is a boom that is backed up by performance. A good example of this is the tiny emirate of Dubai.

Dubai belongs to a country that is composed of seven separate kingdoms. These kingdoms together form the United Arab Emirates (UAE) and the country has been in existence in its present form since 1971. From that time till 2000, the emirate of Dubai was a stopover town between two other kingdoms, a glorified rest stop of sorts (Brook, 2016).

Things changed around 1995 with the appointment of a new crown prince. Quickly things began moving in the sleepy emirate. First, a fancy new hotel called the Burj al Arab was constructed by the coastline. Its design is considered futuristic to this day, so one can imagine the splash it caused when it was completed in 1999.

Property construction began in earnest and land values began booming. At the turn of the millennium, when Western economies were being affected by the dotcom crash, Dubai's economy was about to enter a rapid bull market. A man-made island in the shape of a palm was constructed and investment poured in.

There was justification for this boom. The government was rapidly expanding and modernizing its economy and tourism was growing almost tenfold every year. From 2002 to 2008, property values quadrupled. Given that the kingdom's economy was not tied to oil prices, this was some achievement.

The only comparable boom like the one Dubai has witnessed occurred during the Second Industrial Revolution back in the late 1800s and early 1900s. This was when Germany under Bismarck and the United States rapidly industrialized and joined the big boys' table.

Germany is particularly notable because in the matter of a decade it went from being a primarily agrarian economy to a fully industrialized one. While it faced a lot of hostility from its European neighbors, this hostility was a mark of how potent Germany's boom was.

Justified Bullishness

Technology has fostered huge booms since the turn of the millennium. While there was a massive devaluation in between, this was primarily because of large misunderstandings when it came to value. Companies such as Amazon and Netflix survived the dotcom bust primarily thanks to their businesses providing consumers with real value.

In the early portion of the previous decade, Google and Facebook grew from fledgling startups to behemoths of the industry. All of these examples, including the ones highlighted previously, have something in common. The products and services that were developed are truly valuable and thus the rise in prices is justified.

One of the key changes that occurs during this time is the perception of value. After all, new services and goods have been created and the definition of value changes. For example, the narrative around business valuation before technology companies began to dominate was that profits drove valuation.

However, Facebook and Amazon proved that it was not profits but users that drove valuation. The result was the creation of a completely different philosophy of investing. Where investors once looked at profits and margins, they were now looking at user numbers and growth and didn't care about profits.

A lot of people found this incongruous. How could a business not care about profits at all? Over time, this philosophy has fleshed itself out more and the connection between users and profits is now well established. However, it took everyone a while to get there!

This period is also home to a large number of innovations that facilitate change. For example, the early 2000s saw the transformation of a boring financial derivative called the mortgage bond into a driver of profits. The mortgage bond market was pretty boring at the best of times (Lewis, 2008).

However, between 2003 and 2007, Wall Street banks turned this relatively unknown instrument into the very basis upon which their businesses were founded. This was done in reaction to the great prosperity that Americans were experiencing and the availability of easy money.

Notice that in all of these examples, the transition from the first stage to this one is different. In the case of Dubai and Germany, the process played out over a few years. In the case of the internet companies, it took close to a decade. With mortgage bonds, it took less than two years.

The key is to identify the qualities that underlie these phases instead of getting caught up in how long the stage lasts.

STAGE THREE: BUBBLE

The bubble phase is characterized by euphoria. The bull market has been going on for so long that no one remembers the bad times anymore. People can get adjusted to riches pretty quickly! As a result, complacency sets in because money becomes easier to make.

All of these disruptive companies or sectors have long since moved from being risky to can't-miss territory. The general public now becomes aware that they can make lots of money by investing in certain sectors or in certain assets. A good example of this is provided by the tulip mania that gripped the Netherlands in the early 1600s.

Tulips were viewed as an exotic flower, given that they had to be imported all the way from Istanbul. With prosperity levels growing in the Dutch economy, people began coveting them. Wearing a tulip was a mark of belonging to high society. Soon, Dutch farmers recognized this opportunity (Stage Two) and began growing them.

As people began buying more tulips, the price rose to high levels. The general public caught on to the fact that there was money to be made in tulips and began buying them in bulk to resell them. Soon enough, farmers could not keep up with the demand for tulips and prices skyrocketed (Hayes, 2019).

A secondary market popped up where people sold and bought the rights to buy a tulip. In some cases, the price of the right to buy a tulip was worth more than an entire house. People still bought them though, since there was always someone who would buy it from them.

In short, demand was driven by the fact that there was a greater fool to buy the asset. They were not correlated to the underlying asset's value anymore. Everyone wanted to get in on this thanks to the riches that could be gained and a bubble was formed.

FOMO and Complacency

This stage is mostly characterized by the investing public's fear of missing out and complacency with regards to the disconnect between price and value. The average investor believes that prices can only go up. Pretty much everyone jumps in on the hot new trend because of this.

This decade has witnessed behavior like this. How many people became crypto traders once Bitcoin hit $20,000? How many people bought cryptocurrency at this price in the hopes of making a quick profit? They probably heard stories of someone who bought it at $13,000 and resold it for $18,000 in a few days.

The get-rich-quick mindset prevails during this stage. It's safe to say that this mindset has never made anyone any money. The ones who do manage to make profits usually have luck to thank. This sort of thinking also leads to overvaluations for every asset that closely or even remotely resembles the original disruptor.

Once Bitcoin's price rose sharply, so did the prices of every other cryptocurrency. This led to the rise of a large number of initial coin offerings (ICOs). An ICO is when a new cryptocurrency is launched to prospective investors. The boom in ICO offerings led to outright fraud being perpetrated on the public with shady promoters offering the promise of huge profits with very little justification for them.

The confounding thing is that investors often recognized that there was very little value in the offering but invested their money in them anyway. This highlights the complacency with which they valued the asset to begin with. Everyone was getting into it and the pull of the herd mentality was hard to resist.

The technology world also witnessed some ridiculous overvaluations as well. The social media company Snapchat went public for a price of $24 per share (representing a market cap of $33 billion) despite not having any viable monetization strategy or a platform that lent itself to doing this. As of current writing, the company's stock is still trading at these levels.

A bigger disaster was the massive valuation of the coworking company WeWork. It was thought to be a disruptive company, simply because it positioned itself as being the Uber of office space. At its height, it was valued at $50 billion. The problem was that the company never had a hope of posting a profit. The bigger it got, the larger its losses. What's more, WeWork declared in its SEC filings that it didn't hope to make a profit in the foreseeable future. Currently, it's valued at a far more sober $8 billion.

Zoom was another company whose valuation rose to an eye-watering 63 times revenue (note that's not 63x earnings, we're talking purely on sales numbers). This was despite the fact that the company had never turned a profit. Pretty much everyone jumped in on Zoom and other tech companies because it's what everyone was doing!

Divergence from Fundamentals

At this point you may hear maxims such as

"Value investing doesn't work any more"

"If you'd have just bought every tech IPO in the past 10 years, you'd have outperformed the S&P 500"

"Warren Buffett has lost his touch"

All of these are rooted in a certain degree of truth. However, just because something works in the short term, does not make it a reliable method for the long-term.

As a rule of thumb, if you ever hear the dumbest person you know begin to talk about stocks and the market, that's the time for you to get out.

Another factor in the FOMO-driven stage of the cycle is leverage. Leverage rises massively during these times as people borrow money to get in on the excitement. This is what happened in the case of Dubai's economic boom as well.

By 2008, demand for property was so high that people could buy property and flip it within a month. Developers began waiving down payment requirements since speculators were interested in flipping properties to someone else, without having any interest in owning them. Thus, a person only needed to make a single monthly payment to receive the title to the property.

Such behavior was justified due to the fact that prices were constantly increasing. banks began providing personal loans that were duly used to purchase multiple properties through low monthly payments. Sellers knew that no buyer had any intention of using the property, but they didn't care. All that mattered was the fact that everyone else was doing the same thing.

Smart Money Exits

The bubble stage is when smart money exits the market. Remember that retail investors are also a portion of the smart money group, just as institutional investors can be dumb money. Since the disconnect between value and price is unjustified, these investors recognize the warning signs and cash out their investments.

This is mostly done because having cash during bad times is a huge advantage. It allows an investor to quickly seize opportunities and invest in them while the rest of the market is reeling from the shock of the drop. At this stage the bubble hasn't burst yet, but savvy investors are getting ready for it.

Having said that, even the smartest of investors can get caught in these bubbles. Warren Buffett and Charlie Munger were famously caught out by the credit crisis despite seeing the signs. They managed to steer clear of subprime mortgages in their insurance businesses but didn't foresee the damage that some of their portfolio companies such as Wells Fargo and Moody's took. Recently, they managed to lose money investing in airline companies as well.

STAGE FOUR: EXTERNAL SHOCKS

This stage is when the bubble pops. Just as every great party ends with an external force stopping it dead in its tracks (the lights come on or the cops show up), the bubble is burst by an exogenous event. The shock itself might have nothing to do with economic events, but it causes markets to tumble and it gives pessimists an excuse to begin dumping stocks.

Given the huge disparity that has been created between price and value, there isn't much propping these eye-watering valuations up. As a result, a crisis ensues where prices begin tumbling downwards. Something that catches out a lot of investors is trying to predict what the shock will be, instead of preparing for the occurrence of a shock.

In other words, some investors try to time their exit from the market by looking for signs of specific events that indicate a fall. This is a lot like trying to time your entry into the market. It's a pretty pointless game to take part in since you can never predict what will cause a shock.

The current COVID-19 pandemic is a great example of this. The markets had been fueled by cheap money for a while. While the pandemic caused businesses to shut down, the state to which things have fallen shows how overvalued assets were.

Consider that the American unemployment rate is currently a few points below what it was during the Great Depression (Iacurci, 2020)! The unemployment rate spiked from 2% to 20% in just a few months. It's hard to fathom how this could have happened without businesses being overly reliant on cheap debt that was widely available.

Previous economic crises have also had seemingly innocuous beginnings. The credit crisis of the previous decade is thought to have begun when an obscure hedge fund that was run by Bear Stearns failed in late 2007. To the outside world, no one knew what The High Grade Fund was or what it did, but it began a snowball that would eventually claim its parent firm and a few other notable ones.

The odds of the average investor or even the average institutional investor being able to predict this event as the catalyst for collapse is pretty remote.

Leverage

This stage is marked by the failure of overleveraged companies. Leverage here refers to debt that companies carry on their balance sheets. During the previous stage, companies often borrow cash to finance their businesses. This decade has witnessed unprecedented amounts of leverage being used in

American businesses.

After the credit crisis dissipated in 2009, the government began printing money in order to provide lenders with more money. This was followed by Quantitative Easing (QE) measures. QE is a fancy name for the American government buying toxic assets from lenders to prevent them from going bankrupt.

The money to buy these assets came from newly printed dollar bills. This approach was followed by pretty much every central bank in the world. In an effort to kickstart their economies, interest rates were cut to the bone, with Europe even experiencing negative interest rates.

This created an environment where businesses borrowed money for next to nothing to finance their businesses. While some level of debt is good on a balance sheet, cheap money led to excessive levels of debt being carried. In the past, such levels of debt would have resulted in companies going bankrupt.

However, these days governments have shown that they're willing to step in and prevent the collapse of companies. A good example of this was the sale of Bear Stearns that was orchestrated by the U.S Government. The propping up of RBS by the UK government is another example.

It isn't just the financial sector that has been propped up. The likes of General Motors and Chrysler also received bailout money from the government. While bailouts are a recent phenomenon, this particular stage is characterized by some spectacular bankruptcies, thanks to leverage.

Bear Stearns was bought out by J.P Morgan with the government's assistance, but the firm was allowed to fail as much as possible. The firm became aware of the risks it was running in late 2007 but as the value of its assets dipped, its leverage levels became alarming. A week before it went bankrupt, the stock was trading as high as $100 per share.

Another spectacular collapse from that time was Lehman Brothers. In this case, the government did not intervene and allowed it to fail. Lehman's fall was also characterized by huge levels of leverage. While this was the reason on the surface of it, the real reason was massively overvaluing the assets it was carrying. This was the case with Bear as well.

This overvaluation of assets occurred primarily because both companies were still caught up in the frenzy of the previous stage. They honestly believed they could sell worthless mortgage bond-backed derivatives to other investors and carried these assets on their books for the prices they thought they could get.

Much like the investors who placed their money in the rights to buy tulips, they soon found out that the underlying assets were worthless and the money they had borrowed to buy them was now due.

The same pattern is playing out now with the COVID-19 crisis. A large number of businesses have had to let go of staff and shut down because of not being able to service the debt on their balance sheets. While there hasn't been any high profile bankruptcy yet (other than Hertz) as of this writing, highly leveraged balance sheets might cause further bailouts and even more money printing.

STAGE FIVE: DISGUST

As reality sets in, we will witness people come to terms with what's going on. The financial media, which is ever present to jump into hysterical overreaction, begins using terms such as "worst crisis" and "lowest point in history" and so on.

None of them pointed out or even came close to uncovering what was going on during the previous stages but now, all of a sudden, they begin talking about how the signs were always there. They trot out the appropriate talking heads on their shows and manufacture outrage at how things could get so bad.

New celebrities are born. These are people who managed to correctly call the bubble. The most notable example of this in the previous recession was Michael Burry, whose work was the basis for the book (and subsequent movie) *The Big Short*. Burry was an obscure Hedge Fund manager who rose to prominence in the late 2000s after his Scion Capital firm made investors more than $700m after betting against the sub-prime mortgage bonds which caused the Financial crisis. Burry's fund returned 489.34% in an 8 year period compared to 3% for S&P 500. Burry himself argued that many people had access to the same data he had, and that he was not merely a "supremely lucky flipper of coins." (Burry, 2010).

This is also the time when the tide truly runs out and fraud is uncovered. Following the credit crisis, the biggest scandal that emerged was Bernie Madoff's. Madoff had been running the world's largest Ponzi scheme, which defrauded investors of more than $64 Billion.

The previous recession, the dotcom bust, was also followed by one of the biggest frauds of all time being uncovered in Enron. This was a company that was supposed to be the smartest in the energy trading markets and it turned out that everything had been falsified. What was worse was that the management of the company (chairman Kenneth Lay and the CFO Jeff Skilling) had been dumping company stock while telling their employees to buy more.

The scandal even managed to sink the firm that had audited Enron's books, Arthur Andersen. The damage to their reputation was so bad that they had to change their company's name to Accenture. All of these bleak news items lead to massive distrust in the government and in the established political order.

Following the previous bear market in 2009 we saw protests break out demanding reform. Movements such as Occupy Wall Street began and the common investor, who has probably lost their shirt by now in the markets, was ruminating over how they had been duped by the system.

The stock market is unfair and is loaded against the little guy, such investors think. All this while, the smart money has read the signs and is identifying opportunities that will soon make themselves known.

Prices of companies will be at lows. These might not be historical lows, but they certainly will be near five to 10-year lows. This results in a number of great companies being sold for a fraction of their true value, and slowly but surely, we return to the first stage all over again.

We should note that these five stages describe the overall economy. However, individual sectors will run at their own pace. For example, technology might be experiencing a stage five crisis but healthcare might be in stage three.

When buying individual stocks, it's important for you to focus on the economic cycle that a particular stock or sector is subject to, instead of worrying about the broader economic cycle.

"INVESTORS HAVE LOST MORE MONEY BY TRYING TO ANTICIPATE CORRECTIONS, THAN THEY'VE LOST IN THE CORRECTIONS THEMSELVES"

- Peter Lynch

2
BEAR MARKET TIMELINES AND EMOTIONAL MANAGEMENT

This book is going to focus on stages three to five of the cycle from the previous chapter. A common mistake that many investors make is to fall into the trap of trying only to value a company with as much accuracy as possible. The truth is, it's far more important to control your emotions during such times.

No matter how rational you are or how aware you are of your emotional state, it's tough to go against your evolutionary instincts. If the whole world tells you that things are going to pieces, you're going to believe this to a certain extent. Your investment decisions will reflect this as well.

Recall from the introduction that most investors earn abysmal returns because they end up making the wrong asset allocation decisions. They end up buying when they should be selling and selling when they ought to be buying. Your objective is to maximize your good decisions in bull markets and minimize your bad ones in bear markets.

It's a simple thought process, but it works brilliantly. It helps you focus on avoiding large errors when times are bad. This alone will keep you from making a bad situation worse and will put you in a better situation to take advantage of the bounce that will inevitably occur as the market moves back to stage one of the cycle.

There are a few points you can keep in mind to help you maintain this framework.

THIS IS NOT THE END

During bad times you're going to hear a lot about how everything is going to fall to pieces and how we're all going to go back to a hunter-gatherer society.

There will even be a group of people who will actively look forward to this and they're bound to receive more exposure in the media.

This will lead you to think that the established paradigms of this world are coming to an end. A common thread through all financial crises that have occurred in the United States has been the thought that America is no longer the force it once was. In 1929, the Great Depression was thought to have dampened the fastest growing economy in the world. Following the crash, common thought was that all the economic power America had gained over Europe following World War I had been squandered.

This sentiment carried on throughout the following two to three years until the recovery began in 1933. As we know now the Great Depression, even as bad as it was at the time, was just a very large speed bump in America's ascension to the top of the economic pile.

Doomsday predictions are a dime a dozen during the final stage and you should be very conscious of avoiding that train of thought. Yes, it might look like you'll need to stockpile food and other necessities, but this hardly means you'd be justified in doing so. The current COVID-19 pandemic has proved this over and over again.

When the disease first broke out in China, the rest of the world reacted by dismissing it as nothing more vicious than the flu. As the disease spread and its true ramifications came to be known, people began panicking and storing up on supplies. Even governments began overreacting and implemented lockdowns in ham-fisted ways.

The government of India gave its citizens all of four hours to prepare for a 21-day lockdown (Kettleman & Schultz, 2020). This led to panic buying and gave businesses no time to prepare for the increased demand as consumers stockpiled necessary goods. It also led to large quantities of essential provisions stuck at state borders due to lack of communication between local governments.

In the United States, the President went from suggesting that the disease was nothing to be worried about, to insisting that all Americans lock themselves down to defeat the virus, to refusing to wear a mask, to suggesting that people inject disinfectants, to inciting people to rebel against local government lockdowns, to vowing to reopen America. The world anxiously awaits the next stage of this sequence.

Throughout all of this, what has been missed is that human beings are remarkably adaptable. Across the world, people have adapted to new circumstances and have gone on with their lives. While there's no denying that times are tough, a lot of the hysteria that has been generated has prevented people from focusing on the few positives that have emerged.

The world is not going to go back to the Stone Age. So relax and focus on what's truly important to you.

THE LONG-TERM APPROACH

What does short-term or long-term mean to you? To some people the short term signifies the next few weeks. For some particularly fast-paced folks, it could mean the next few hours. It's important to gain the right perspective when it comes to these terms and investing.

In order to be successful at investing, you need to focus on the long term. How long is the long term? This is typically at least a decade long. Your money needs time to grow and it works best when you stand aside and let it compound. Interfering with it constantly by reacting to short-term news cycles is only going to decrease its growing power.

How long is the short term? By stock investing standards, the short term refers to the next two years at the very least. Remember that successful stock investment is not like trading, where you jump in and out of stocks repeatedly. You need to buy and hold for long periods of time in order to allow your investments to grow.

This is because in the long term, a company's stock price grows at the same rate that its earnings do. Like Benjamin Graham said, in the short term the market is a voting machine, but in the long term, it's a weighing machine ("The Voting and Weighing Machines," 2020). You'll need to overcome a variety of short-term sentiments for the long-term trend to assert itself.

A good illustration of this occurred when the credit crisis was beginning to unfold in 2007. Things were falling apart, and in the middle of all this Warren Buffett repeated his oft-quoted investment mantra for the common investor in his annual letter to Berkshire Hathaway shareholders: Buy a cross section of America and hold.

What Buffett meant was that even at the height of pessimistic opinion, the average investor needed to simply invest in an index fund that would give them exposure to the broad stock market. He even said that this simple investment would outperform the best hedge fund over the next decade (Floyd, 2019).

To put this in context, Buffett made this statement when home prices were tumbling across the nation and firms such as Countrywide Financial were in danger of going under. No one fully knew the extent of the crisis and how bad things would get. There wasn't even talk of a bailout yet! The climate was grim and many people around the country were being foreclosed on.

Buffett's bet was taken up by Protege Partners, a hedge fund based in New York, and the terms of the bet were modified a bit. Buffett would place $1 million of his own money into a low-cost index fund that tracked the S&P 500 broad stock market index while Protege would invest the same amount in a basket of hedge funds.

As 2007 turned to 2008, Buffett's investment was hammered. The market kept tumbling to new lows. By mid 2008, the market had tumbled 20% and it kept getting worse. By mid 2009, Buffett had lost 50% of his original value. Protege partners did very well during this time.

The exact numbers are not known, but their basket of funds earned an admirable 10% during this time. When compared to a tumble of close to 50% in the overall market, this was a stellar return indeed. It seemed as if Buffett was wrong to back a simple and cost-effective strategy.

Fast forward to 2017 and Buffett's simple investment had averaged 7% per year while the hedge fund basket had averaged just 2.2% per year. What's more, Protege Partners had given up the bet in 2015, conceding defeat and remarking that there was no way they could hope to beat Buffett's bet within the short time remaining on the bet!

This is remarkable considering the head start that the hedge fund basket had in the beginning. Buffett likened this scenario to the famous fable about the hare and the tortoise. While the hedge funds practiced a form of investing much like the hare, by jumping around into different asset classes and looking to time their entries into the market perfectly, Buffett's tortoise-like bet simply stayed the course and remained steady.

In the end, he came out ahead, just like the tortoise does in the fable. Without the clarity that focusing on the long term brings, this would not have been possible.

Rallies

During bear markets, at some point the news cycle shifts from pure outrage at the state of events to hope. Market observers begin to hype good news and celebrate every single uptick in the market. You'll often hear news such as "markets rallied 21% this month to finish their best month since the crisis" and so on.

While such news might give investors some solace, the fact is that they conceal more than they reveal. Let's consider an example to demonstrate how this works. We're going to highlight some sample returns the market provided within a three-year period. The time in which the returns below are earned are different.

In some cases, the return is earned over a month and in some it's six months. Whatever the timeline is, take a look at these numbers and ask yourself: Do these numbers make it seem as if the entire market is bullish or bearish over the course of these three years?

- 48% gain
- 12% gain
- 21% gain
- 27% gain
- 35% gain
- 72% gain

You'd be forgiven for thinking these came during a bull market. In fact these returns were earned during the worst three-year stretch that American markets have ever faced. That's right! Our sample three-year period runs from the height of 1929 right before the crash till 1932, which is when the market hit the bottom.

The market during this time lost 90% of its value. $10 invested in the beginning of this period would have been worth just $1 at the end of it. But just looking at those gain numbers, you don't get the feeling that they could have been produced during one of the worst times in American stock market history, do they?

This is precisely how rallies are reported in the media. A rally refers to an upward movement in a bearish market. Markets don't decline in a straight line. They go up and down, with the longer-term trend being down. The media might breathlessly report those numbers, especially the 72% rally, and give you the impression that the worst is over.

However, they neglect to mention that the market has declined by close to 90% from its highs and that the 72% rally is measured from the most recent low. For example, let's say the market price is currently $70 and that it has declined from a high of $350 to this level. That's a decline of 80%.

Before it rose to $70, the market had made a low of $40.70 and has now rallied to the $70 price. This is a rally of 72%. Clearly, it barely takes anything out of the overall decline. Don't get carried away by such gaudy rally numbers. The way they're measured causes investors to lose sight of the big picture.

By the way, those numbers aren't made up. They're real numbers that the Dow Jones Index hit between 1929 to 1932. The 72% rally was a rise from a low of around 41 to around 72. The index fell to these levels from a high of 380.

UNCERTAINTY AND OPPORTUNITY

Information is widely available these days. Be it on social media or through websites such as Seeking Alpha, you can access credible research reports on any company out there. There are also a large number of research firms that operate entirely on the internet, and by subscribing to their newsletters, you can access quality research material on everything from microcap stocks to behemoths.

This is a double-edged sword. You have huge access to this treasure trove of information. However, so does everyone else. The news that you've read in your newsletter has been read by other subscribers as well. If enough people get there ahead of you, the price of a company's stock will rise or fall to reflect its intrinsic value. It might even become overpriced.

This has led many market spectators to posit that the markets these days are far too efficient. The Efficient Market Hypothesis (EMH) has been around for a long time. EMH is a theoretical financial principle that says that all information surrounding a business (and its stock) have already been factored into its price.

For example, if Walmart is expected to announce bumper earnings, the price at which its stock sells in the market will be priced to reflect this fact ahead of time. As a result, when the bumper earnings announcement does come through, the stock won't witness a huge jump upwards.

EMH has always been used as a model to figure out the intrinsic value of a stock and plays an important role in valuation models that are a part of corporate finance courses. So what does all this have to do with you? It turns out that EMH has been a pretty terrible way to value stocks for a long time now.

This is primarily because information has never been widely available about a company in the past. A company in China that sells fertilizer and is listed on the New York Stock Exchange is unlikely to have its price account for all factors affecting the business. There's just too much of a gap.

To be more accurate, we should say there *was* too much of a gap. As information has become more freely available, market prices have become more efficient. The speed of the average market transaction has increased exponentially and, as a result, prices adjust to available information quickly.

In an efficient world, the only way to gain an advantage is to spot inefficiency. During normal times, doing this is close to impossible. Everyone is in the market and everyone is paying attention to all relevant news items. The number of casual market participants is high and institutional presence is also high. Thus, the average investor doesn't have much time to capture any inefficiencies.

An underreported company's stock might sell at a discount for a short period of time, but that mispricing isn't going to last for long since word will get out, and quickly. This dynamic changes during a bear market.

During these times, markets are a bit more inefficient. This is because the primary nature of news is pessimistic and no one likes listening to Debbie Downer. The average investor has probably witnessed their principal reduce massively and is therefore disinclined to take further part in the market.

In short, everyone's hurting and this is where your opportunity arises. There will be inefficiencies present in every sector and your task is simply to filter the news that is available. The saturation of information works to your advantage in these times because fewer people are willing to act upon it.

Successful bear market investing requires you to adopt a contrarian approach. You might believe that overcoming your inbuilt psychological mechanisms might be impossible. However, if you adopt this mindset of looking for diamonds in the rough when everyone else has given up, you'll manage to invest your money successfully.

Another important element of success is to avoid the traps that many investors fall into. These traps can come in the form of extremely negative news. It can also come in the form of flat-out misjudgment of the opportunity that's presented to you. You need to monitor your actions and be aware of your biases at all times.

While this isn't easy, viewing uncertainty as an opportunity for you to get ahead reduces your risk of making a mistake.

OVERVALUING BOUNCES

Previously we addressed this topic in brief, and it's worth taking a deeper look. The real reason the media and commentators scream with joy every time the market bounces is because people get used to trading in one direction. As long as things are going up, our brains are happy because their reward centers are being stimulated.

The minute things start going down, alarm bells start ringing and it feels physically uncomfortable for us to watch what's going on. During the COVID-19 pandemic, we've seen the effects of this discomfort. People have been pushing to get the American economy open quickly and get things back on track as soon as possible.

While livelihoods are at stake, the idea of making the pandemic go away just by reopening the economy is a head scratcher. Are governments and their people really willing to risk lives in order to reduce the unemployment rate? While there are significant numbers of people who are suffering, surely a more balanced approach is needed.

This mindset has led to a skewed manner in which market movements are reported. The markets declined precipitously in February and March 2020 as the world grappled with the true extent of the virus. April saw a huge rally and this was reported as being almost as if the crisis had come to an end.

However, the rally represents less than half the drop the market suffered from its highs. The fact is that such overly bullish news is great for retail investors. It simply means the opposite is happening and that there are great opportunities for you to unearth.

IRRATIONALITY IN THE MARKETS

John Maynard Keynes, one of the few economists who was also a successful investor, remarked that the markets can remain irrational longer than the investor can remain solvent (O'Brien, 2012). Investigating this quote a little bit more provides us with a cautionary piece of advice that every bear market investor must pay heed to.

Keynes, whose career spanned the decades before and after the Great Depression, was famous for remarking that the stock market was a lot like a beauty contest. Imagine a contest where you had to pick the six best-looking contestants out of 10 on stage. The catch is that you don't win a prize unless the large crowd agrees with your picks.

Success in this contest thus depends on how popular your picks are, irrespective of whether you believe your picks represent the six best-looking people. Stocks are pretty much the same. Their valuations are often driven by euphoria, and towards the end of bubbles many rational investors lose sight of this.

They believe that the bubble must have run its course and that the existing valuations are too far removed from reality. As a result, they begin to act upon their biases and fail to recognize one simple fact. Their opinion doesn't count unless the market backs it up. The markets, as Keynes pointed out, can remain irrational for far longer than one can expect.

With regards to present market conditions, consider that there have been voices remarking that the market was overvalued all the way back in 2016.

Bill Gross, the famous bond investor and trader, is one such example (Heaton, 2016). Gross was in fact bearish on the economy since 2014!

Considering that the market was exhibiting signs of overheating all the way back then and is turning bearish in 2020, one can appreciate just how much patience and room for error there is when it comes to investing in bear markets. An investor who built their entire investment thesis without taking irrationality into account would have probably lost patience long before the markets began nosediving.

In some cases, bad news might come pouring in yet the stock price continues to rise. There's also the danger of underestimating irrationality after an initial fall. You might see the stock price fall and heave a sigh of relief thanks to expecting this for a long time. However, the price might immediately recover and continue back up to make new highs.

The markets are unpredictable and this makes it extremely important that you always cover your downside. This means you need to ground your investment thesis in facts and not according to your biases. Extreme rationality is also a bias. You're effectively saying that every participant in the market is rational and always acts on the basis of provided information.

This is a lot like what EMH hypothesizes and it's never fully worked despite some of its tenets proving true in recent times. It sounds strange to say this, but your investment process must take irrationality into account. Both your own and that of the other investors in the market.

"TRUTH - MORE PRECISELY, AN ACCURATE UNDERSTANDING OF REALITY - IS THE ESSENTIAL FOUNDATION FOR PRODUCING GOOD OUTCOMES."

Ray Dalio, who started Bridgewater Associates in his apartment. It became the world's largest hedge fund within 25 years.

THE ONION - ADOPTING THE RATIONAL PROCESS INVESTING MODEL FOR A BEAR MARKET

So what is Rational Process Investing anyway? More importantly, how can you create a process to serve you through both bullish and bearish markets? The best way to think of this process is to use an analogy Jim Chanos regularly uses when he teaches investment at Yale and the University of Wisconsin (Koster, 2018). With regards to your long-term investing process, this is the most important piece of information in this book, so make sure you understand it thoroughly.

Chanos likens the company analysis process to peeling away the layers of an onion. Most investors begin from the outside in. They peel the outer layers of the onion and then progressively go towards the inner core. Presumably by the time they reach the inner kernel of the onion, they're weeping their eyes out and don't take their time with it.

According to Chanos, intelligent analysis is done the other way around. The investor needs to work from the inside out. They need to begin with the most painful part of the process and then progressively move towards the less tearful bits.

In Chanos' analogy, the inner core of the onion contains the information provided by the company that cannot be fudged. These are the 10-K filings along with other legally mandated filings that every public company has to provide to the SEC.

One layer removed from this inner core are the press releases put out by the company. These are fairly reliable, but their tone and message can be gilded, depending on how well the PR firm handling the issue massages words. Companies will typically not lie outright in these, but this doesn't mean that everything presented is 100% true either.

The third layer is the earnings calls that management conducts with analysts. These calls are usually held right after earnings announcements are made. Here, investors can listen to analysts that cover the company ask management questions about certain areas of their business and financials.

These statements are then used by analysts to create company analysis reports and these form the fourth layer of the onion. By the time this report has been published, it contains a ton of projections and estimates that may or may not be true. Most anomalies in reports have been explained away by management and analysts tend to toe the line with what management says.

The final layer of the onion is your neighbor Bob. Bob does nothing but trawl social media all day and isn't afraid to let people know his stock recommendations. He's a self-proclaimed expert on the financial markets despite his experience with it amounting to standing next to the Broadway bull. Your family members and all of your social media contacts fall into the Bob category.

Unfortunately, this is where most people begin and end their investing journey. Instead of doing this, do the intelligent thing and begin with the deepest, most uncomfortable, yet most accurate layer.

We should note, that simply hearing about a company on social media or from family and friends is not in itself a bad thing. The issue arises when buying decisions are made solely from this layer five level "research", if you can even call it research.

No matter where you hear about a company or potential investment, start at layer one and work your way outwards. We'll now explain each layer in depth.

LAYER ONE—LEGALLY MANDATED FILINGS

Why should you start with these filings instead of say, the analyst calls or research reports? Think of it this way: By reading these reports, you're getting the worst-case scenario in many ways. This is because the SEC thoroughly regulates the language contained within these filings.

Companies cannot conceal any facts or exaggerate any other elements in their financials unless it happens to be an opinion. Such opinions are noted explicitly in these filings. Do note that not all legal filings fall into this category.

Wall Street gets pretty breathless covering 10-Q releases. The 10-Q is a quarterly earnings statement that is filed by all public companies. It contains all of the financial information pertaining to the business in that quarter. Sounds pretty important, doesn't it? There's just one catch.

10-Qs are not audited! The company can literally enter any figure and pass it off as real. If the number is completely nonsensical, companies will release an amended 10-Q that contains a more realistic number. However, for analysis purposes, 10-Qs should be taken with a grain of salt.

The report that investors should be reading is the 10-K. These are the annual report filings that companies make with the SEC.

The 10-K

Do not confuse the 10-K filing with the annual reports that you can find on companies' investor relations websites. The latter are slickly produced and contain a large dose of propaganda. The SEC filing on the other hand is dull as ditchwater and looks like every high school student's worst nightmare.

It contains many pages, doesn't have any pictures and is written in small type. It also contains language that is forcefully neutral and is filled with legalese in certain areas. It has paragraphs that go on and on and is seemingly written by the most boring person in the world.

All of this is great news for you!

Believe it or not, this dull language serves a very important purpose. It stops you from getting carried away in the euphoria surrounding a company. There are a number of sections that do this brilliantly in a 10-K. The first section that is invaluable in a 10-K is the "Business" section.

This is where a company discusses their history and explains their business in detail. If they happen to have a subdivision of a subdivision hidden away in Wichita, you'll learn about it here. Companies can get a bit one-eyed over here and talk themselves up a bit.

To tone this down, the SEC mandates that the "Risk Factors" section come next. This section lays out all of the worst-case scenarios facing a business.

For example, here are some gems from market favorite Tesla's 10-K (Tesla, 2020):

- *Any problems or delays in expanding Gigafactory Nevada or ramping and maintaining operations there, could negatively affect the production and profitability of our products, such as Model 3, Model Y and our energy storage products. In addition, the battery cells produced there store large amounts of energy.*
- *Any issues or delays in meeting our projected timelines, costs and production at or funding the ramp of Gigafactory Shanghai, or any difficulties in generating and maintaining local demand for vehicles manufactured there, could adversely impact our business, prospects, operating results and financial condition.*

Both of these points explained a lot of Elon Musk's latest tweets surrounding the lockdown. Mind you, these are just the headings of these sections. The company expands on both of these points in a lot of detail within the report.

Last but not least is this item:

- *We are highly dependent on the services of Elon Musk, our Chief Executive Officer.*

There are many ways of interpreting that particular line. On one hand you could argue that Musk's personality is the company's biggest strength. On the other hand, for a company of Tesla's size to be so heavily dependent on one man could be concerning. This book isn't providing stock recommendations, so we'll just leave it at that.

Our point is that you're unlikely to read such things in the company's press releases and certainly not in Musk's tweets. The company has to disclose all of its risk factors to investors. In addition to this, it also has to list all legal proceedings that it currently faces as well as all property it owns or leases.

The next section that is highly informative comes a little later in the report. This is titled the "Auditor's Report" or some equivalent name. This is where the auditing firm provides an opinion about the veracity of the financial statements as well as its opinions about the company's finances. It also highlights any accounting changes that have been made recently.

For example, here is what PricewaterhouseCoopers LLP notes about Tesla's financial statements:

As discussed in Note 2 to the consolidated financial statements, the Company changed the manner in which it accounts for leases in 2019 and the manner in which it accounts for revenue from contracts with customers in 2018.

This by itself is not an alarming note by any means since companies do this often. However, it alerts the investor to take a look at Note 2 in order to understand the basis of these statements better. Again, this isn't something you'll learn about by following social media.

Then there are the financial statements themselves that provide a lot of insight into a company's situation. Management discusses and highlights some of these numbers in a separate section that is quite illuminating as well.

Overall, the 10-K contains a wealth of information that every serious investor must read. It's best to read 10-Ks going back a few years since this gives a better picture of how the company has evolved over time.

Despite the high level of transparency in the 10-K, there are a few things to watch out for and pay attention to.

Notes to the Statements

The notes to statements are often treated much in the same way the bibliography of a book is treated by the average reader. Naming this section as being the "notes" is unfortunate. A better name, such as "the keys to understanding the statements" might get more investors to read them.

The notes are where companies are required to come clean about every little thing on their financial statements. This is where they describe their revenue recognition process, explain how they accounted for various line items and explain all off balance sheet financing measures.

That final term is something that Jeff Skilling of Enron was particularly fond of, and Enron was disclosing its less-than-honest scheme of earnings recognition in the notes of its 10-K long before the general public got wind of it (Ponzio, 2007).

The notes are also particularly illuminating when it comes to looking at the stock options that are being awarded to management. These days, stock options are expensed from income, but this wasn't always the case in the past. While you don't need to worry about excessive stock option awards these days, it pays to take a look at the sort of incentives management is being offered.

The notes also contain special items that are relevant to the way in which the company has accounted for certain one-off charges. You don't have to be an expert in accounting to understand these items. While they are heavy with jargon, they're not as difficult to understand as a lot of investors think.

Often, the notes will contain amendments to revenues that the company has recognized. This typically happens when the company has taken advantage of certain revenue recognition loopholes. SEC rules mandate that companies clarify all of the instances of this. The notes are where they disclose them and unfortunately most investors don't read them.

Revenues and earnings are at the center of a lot of controversy when it comes to accounting principles. These are the next topic of our discussion.

GAAP and EBITDA

Businesses are complex things and companies typically have complicated revenue streams. For example, when should a company recognize revenues on their books? For a small business, it makes sense to recognize them when cash enters their bank account. However, it's not so simple in the case of a large business.

Let's take the case of a retailer. They might have sold goods in December, yet face a raft of returns in February, thanks to a 90-day refund policy. Assuming their financial year ends in December, a cash-based revenue recognition system would result in massive ups and downs. It won't paint a clear picture of the way the company earns money.

Another example is that of companies that make sales towards the end of quarters or reporting periods. Let's say they land a huge account a few days before the reporting period ends. The customer is surely going to pay, but their cash will arrive a few days after the period ends. For all intents and purposes, the money is in the bank.

If a cash-based recognition system is followed, this will skew the numbers between the two reporting periods. You'll see a large peak in one period preceded by a much smaller peak or even a trough. Some companies receive payments for services a few years down the road thanks to payment plans and other agreements they have with their customers.

All of this makes revenue recognition a headache for companies. This also happens to be just one of many accounting issues that they deal with. To solve these issues a bunch of smart accountants got together and created a set of principles called the Generally Accepted Accounting Principles or GAAP (Tuovila, 2020).

GAAP is a lot like democracy. It isn't perfect, but it's the least worst system we have. There are loopholes in the GAAP framework and the SEC recognizes them. This is partly why the notes to the statements exist. GAAP rules are widely used in North America while the rest of the world follows the International Financial Reporting Standards (IFRS) protocol.

IFRS and GAAP are pretty much the same when it comes down to it. If you're looking at American companies, you'll be dealing with GAAP. One of the biggest grey areas in the GAAP framework is the recognition of revenues. The rules state that revenues must be recognized when there is substantial evidence of the work being complete and of the certainty of payment.

This is up to the discretion of the company and its auditors. The burden of proof is on the company, and the independent auditor must enforce standards when preparing the 10-K. Companies typically don't violate this rule because the consequences of doing so are too large. They could face a public backlash from their investors that sends their stock price tumbling.

Besides, GAAP now mandates companies to release a cash flow statement along with the income statement and balance sheet. The cash flow statement clarifies a lot of points that can be raised with regards to revenue recognition, and as such, there isn't much room to fudge the numbers.

There are a few loopholes, but these can be detected by reading the notes to the statements. The bottom line is that GAAP is a reliable framework for creating complex financial statements. There might be a few issues, but these are handled easily by intelligent investors.

Somewhere in the mid 80s, Wall Street began realizing the huge potential of the investment banking model. Previously, they earned fees only when companies wanted to merge with one another and the primary mode of exchange was equity. Somewhere along the way banks started figuring out that instruments such as junk bonds and convertible debt could be used just as effectively.

As the phenomenon of the leveraged buyout and hostile takeover became more mainstream, these banks ran into a problem. GAAP earnings often posed a problem when it came to financing these takeovers. A typical corporate raider would approach the bank to borrow money (junk bonds) to finance a takeover.

However due to GAAP income being too low or too high, financing would not always pass through a lender's underwriting requirements. The specifics of this process are not important. What you need to understand is that Wall Street, ever considerate of its clients' needs, created a solution.

This solution was called Earnings Before Interest, Taxes, Depreciation and Amortization or EBITDA (pronounced e-bit-da). This is a metric that makes a lot of sense on the surface, but in typical Wall Street fashion the devil is in the details. Here's how the reasoning goes: companies deduct a large number of non-cash-related expenses from their revenues.

Depreciation, for example, is a non-cash charge that companies take to reduce the value of the assets on their books. A desk that you bought five years ago is not worth the same amount you paid for it. You're still using it so you don't know what its market value is. The solution is to reduce its value by a certain percentage until you reduce it to zero.

Amortization works the same way. Let's say you're renting a home and the landlord tells you that you need to pay the entire year's rent before moving in. This will lead to a huge cash hit upfront that will make it seem as if you've run out of money. This is inaccurate. The solution is to report the rental expense as 12 monthly payments over the course of the year. You amortize that single huge expense over time.

Then we have interest and taxes. Wall Street never quite explained the rationale behind including these in EBITDA, but it's included, so let's roll with it. By subtracting all of these non-cash expenses, taxes and interest, you gain a clearer picture of what the company's earning power is. At least that's what the proponents of EBITDA claim.

There is some merit to this. Buffett and Munger have spoken in the past about calculating owner earnings and that calculation also adds back non-cash expenses. However, EBITDA is a very different animal. For one thing, it's a non-GAAP measure.

This means companies are free to fudge it as they please. Here's a brief summary of what can be done (Mercer, 2020):

1. E - Earnings can be recognized for practically anything. If the company signed a memorandum of understanding (MoU - not a sales agreement), they can theoretically recognize that as proof of revenue.
2. I - Interest expense is excluded and this flat-out makes zero sense. It's a bit like saying a person's mortgage, car and credit card payments are not real expenses.
3. DA - These two items are prone to fudging even with GAAP. Companies can accelerate or decelerate their rates of D & A to boost earnings. With GAAP gone, companies can add as much as they please to EBITDA and claim it comes from D & A.

Over and above this, companies can claim any expense they like to cook EBITDA right up to the levels they want it to be. Enron was exemplary in this regard and one wonders what Jeff Skilling might have achieved had he directed his creative skills towards art or music.

Enron regularly hyped its EBITDA numbers and created a buzz on Wall Street. This boosted its stock price and earned its management hefty stock option compensation. A typical model that Skilling used to boost EBITDA was to recognize MoUs as evidence of revenue collection (Segal, 2020).

Of course, this being Jeff Skilling there was an added dash of creativity applied. The MoUs were signed between Enron and offshore subsidiaries of Enron. Imagine if a car maker's Japanese unit agreed to buy cars from its American unit and then cancelled the order once the reporting period passed. This is pretty much what was going on with Enron, amongst other equally nonsensical measures.

EBITDA can be manipulated to the extreme and is a Wall Street creation. It has never made sense and you ought to ignore this. GAAP has a few loopholes but is a far tighter regime. This is what you must pay attention to. 10-K filings are GAAP based.

LAYER TWO—COMPANY PRESS RELEASES

While the 10-K is pretty hard to put a spin on, press releases offer a bit more leeway in this regard. Here companies are bound by regulations from the SEC but have control over the words they use. Thus, with some decent wordsmithing, they can potentially downplay the impact of adverse circumstances.

The size of the company in question also plays a role in how press releases can be used. Smaller companies often use press releases to tout their earnings and this can cause stock prices to rise. There's also selective disclosure that is practiced.

Larger companies have an army of lawyers who protect them from disclosing too much in their releases. The idea is to promote the good and minimize the bad as much as possible. Consider this recent press release from Tesla that is exemplary in its optimism ("Tesla Q1 2020 Vehicle Production & Deliveries," 2020):

In the first quarter, we produced almost 103,000 vehicles and delivered approximately 88,400 vehicles. This is our best ever first quarter performance.

The quarter referenced above is the first quarter of 2020. "Best ever" quarterly performance! Sounds great! The press release continues below.

Model Y production started in January and deliveries began in March, significantly ahead of schedule. Additionally, our Shanghai factory continued to achieve record levels of production, despite significant setbacks.

"Ahead of schedule," "record levels of production"—all of this sounds great. "Significant setbacks"? Well, record production levels offset that! Tesla has seemingly managed to overcome the challenges of a global pandemic.

At least, that's what the management wants you to think. The point here is not to say that Tesla is hiding things. Every company practices this sort of communication. It's important for you to look at what lies beneath these statements.

Note the point about record levels of production from Shanghai. If you glance at the most recent 10-K (reporting results from 2019), Tesla notes that the factory was scheduled to open in January 2020. Thus, "record levels of production" are to be expected in Q1 2020 if there is no previous record to compare it to!

While Tesla's form of communication is the most prevalent, there are instances where companies will simply lie on their press releases. This usually happens when the company is unaware of the situation and is often the result of incompetence and not malice.

A good case in point was the Cambridge Analytica scandal that Facebook was involved in. Facebook data was being used to create user profiles and this was used to deliver targeted political ads to them. Facebook did provide a disclosure saying that users' data might be misused.

However, it adopted a "don't ask, don't tell" policy when it came to data misuse by third-party companies. As far as it was concerned, the way other platforms used data it provided was none of its business. Facebook's argument was a bit like saying that if you lend someone money and they end up causing harm using that money, it isn't your fault.

Except, Facebook knew what Cambridge Analytica was doing with user data. In the previous example, it's like knowing what the other person was planning to do with the money before you gave it to them. This was the basis of the SEC's argument ("Facebook to Pay $100 Million for Misleading Investors About the Risks It Faced From Misuse of User Data," 2019).

Frustratingly, the company got away with a $100 million fine, which barely moves the needle, given its size. It also did not admit any wrongdoing. All Mark Zuckerberg had to do was appear on C-Span and repeat that he was sorry to a group of appropriately outraged senators.

Throughout the scandal, Facebook's press releases touted how it "valued" users' privacy. Once the scandal ended, it announced that it was "turning the page" on the scandal and was focusing on the "future."

LAYER THREE—EARNINGS CALLS WITH MANAGEMENT

Once a company releases earnings reports, it typically holds an earnings call with analysts covering the company. These calls are an opportunity for analysts to question management about the recent results and any other issues that surround the company. In practice, what really happens is that management receives a bunch of softball questions that are easy to handle without saying much of value.

One of the more famous earnings calls transcripts occurred in 2015 when the CEO of Marriott was questioned by an analyst about expected changes to the holiday season spending patterns. The analyst enquired whether there was anything investors ought to know about Q1 2016.

The CEO responded by saying that New Year's Day would fall on January 1st. The CFO responded that Easter would fall on a Sunday. Everyone chuckled and moved on.

The reason for such inanity occurs because analysts are heavily dependent on the very managers of the company they cover. Wall Street analysts are expected to provide thorough and intelligent sounding reports to their clients. However, these reports cannot be thorough without gaining access to company documents.

These documents are provided by management and there is an unspoken quid pro quo that occurs here. If the analyst provides a bad review of the company, you can bet that their levels of access will be curtailed or that important information might be withheld.

It isn't entirely the analysts' fault, to be honest. It's their job to have an opinion. However, not every client appreciates an honest opinion despite what they might say. This is typically the case with hot stocks such as Tesla and Netflix that everyone loves. A sell rating from an analyst usually results in prices dropping.

This enrages existing investors and they direct their ire towards the analyst who made the call. As a result, the analyst loses client support and, coupled with the loss of company access, it's a death knell for their career.

Earnings calls therefore are a meet and greet between old friends. Some companies hold themselves to a high standard of honesty and transparency. The majority of them don't.

LAYER FOUR—WALL STREET ANALYST REPORTS

Despite being a different layer, the same issues plague this layer as well. We're still in the world of the analyst and it's close to impossible to receive an honest opinion from them about the companies they cover. Once the earnings reports have been released and calls done, it's the analyst's job now to put some spin on things.

If everything is fine with the company, the analyst doesn't have much to do. All they need to do is repeat what management says and their job is done. This keeps both the company as well as the clients happy. Things become more difficult when the company is facing a tough time.

In such situations, the analyst relies on future earnings and projections. In particular, there is one nonsensical metric that is often put forward. This is the forward price to earnings ratio (PE). The PE ratio is calculated by dividing the stock price by the earnings per share. It is a measure of how cheap or expensive the company is.

All sectors have different standards by which the PE is defined as being expensive or cheap. Technology companies typically have high PE ratios while utility companies have low PE ratios. The forward PE uses projected earnings per share in its calculation.

To calculate the projected earnings of a company, the analyst uses all kinds of estimates and other data provided by management to arrive at an estimate. The fact that this is an estimate gets lost on them at some point and forward PE ratios are treated as gospel. It's not uncommon to witness stock prices drop after an analyst projects a lower forward PE.

Thus, according to the market and the average investor, a good analyst has to be a psychic as well.

Apart from this projection nonsense that happens, there are deep conflicts of interest that are rife within the industry. Analysts typically work for large investment banks. These investment banks earn hefty fees from companies for carrying out all kinds of work with regards to restructuring, going public etc.

It's a brave analyst who issues a sell rating for a company that is a lucrative client of the highly paid investment banking and trading division. Analysts who do this are immediately sidelined and fade away from the Street after a few years.

Lastly, every analyst has their own system of weighting and standards. A buy rating from one analyst might equate to a hold from another. For example, if analysts from Barrington's Research and C.L. King expect a company to outperform the S&P 500 by 9% over the next year, the former would rate it as a strong buy while the latter would issue a hold rating on it ("Guide to Analyst Recommendations," 2020).

Analyst reports are not completely useless. However, you do need to keep the inherent conflicts of interest and bias in mind when reading them. They can give you insight into select data from within the company. Just don't rely on them entirely and definitely don't pay any attention to ratings.

LAYER FIVE—MAINSTREAM NEWS, SOCIAL MEDIA CHATTER AND STOCK TIPS FROM FRIENDS AND FAMILY

There is a wide variety of media that is contained within this layer. Think of how the average person makes stock investment decisions and you have an example of this layer. Tips from friends and family, your coworker, social media, mainstream media and so on are examples of layer five sources of research.

Calling it research is a bit of a stretch. In this layer there is almost no insight. At best, you might find some funny memes and that's about it. Unfortunately, this layer has an outsized impact on stock price. We say unfortunate because it indicates the number of people who confine themselves here.

As an intelligent investor, this is a huge advantage for you. Social media chatter will lead to some amazing buying opportunities in companies. After all, you cannot receive bargains with inefficiencies existing and social media is one huge inefficiency when it comes to company analysis.

Knee-jerk opinions? Check. Lack of nuance in analysis? Check. A desire to one up the other person instead of solving an issue? Check. These behaviors aren't native to just social media. The mainstream media is adept at this as well. Prominent financial reporters make a name for themselves by breaking news about companies. It's just that the sources of these news items come from within the company itself. There hasn't been any mainstream media outlet that has broken news of fraud or of any other form of financial inappropriateness. Even worse is the habit of financial shows bringing expert investors on the show to lend an air of credibility.

Famous investors typically recommend stocks on air and this ends up driving prices up massively. While the recommendations might be solid, it doesn't change the fact that a company's stock is a bargain at a certain price. Buying a loaf of bread for a few cents is a great deal. Buying it for five dollars is a bit of a stretch.

Opinions at this stage are simply a collection of the herd mentality. You're unlikely to receive any insight here. Even hotshot CEOs who use their Twitter accounts as propaganda tools rarely provide any insight. Elon Musk famously fires off on Twitter all the time.

One tweet of his caused a drop of 10% in Tesla's stock price to $700. The media reported this by saying that $14 billion had been "wiped" off Tesla's market value. Musk is unlikely to have cared because he inhabits another planet and he's unlikely to have sold any of his stock. Intelligent investors spotted an opportunity and Tesla's stock duly hit $1,200 within the next 3 months.

Most investors begin their analysis at this level and work backwards through the layers. By the time they get to the most important layers, they've formed a strong opinion of the company and are now subject to their own confirmation bias. They're looking for evidence that supports their point of view instead of remaining neutral. Herein lies the danger of working from the outside in, rather than the inside out.

A classic example of a level 5 trap is that of Luckin Coffee. The Chinese company was a social media darling for much of 2018 and 2019. A media narrative focused on technological disruption and being dubbed "The Chinese Starbucks", drove stock prices up 20 fold from the IPO price.

However, smart investors would have noticed a lack of transparency in financial reports, dubious claims about how sales were actually recorded (all sales were recorded within the company's own mobile app), and growth numbers which were completely divergent from the "eye-test" of the number of people physically present in Luckin Coffee stores.

So it was of no surprise to us when less than a year after the IPO, Luckin disclosed that 75% of their 2019 revenue was fake. Share prices tumbled 83% in a single day, and it was retail investors who felt the brunt of this (Han, 2020).

This didn't stop many retail investors from sensing a get rich opportunity. So we saw significant buying from retail investors when Luckin hit $5/share. This buying spree wasn't based on fundamentals, or intrinsic value. Instead it was based on greed and hope. We've seen a similar situation with Hertz as well.

Hope is not a process, and imagining that if a stock like Luckin only recovers to 30% of all time highs, you'll still make a huge profit" does not change poor management and bad finances.

We live in the greatest investing age ever. Because anyone with an internet connection can now access the most unbiased financial reporting on any public company within minutes. Therefore, it's imperative your process starts from the inside out, and deals with the most uncomfortable information first. Doing so will not only make you a better investor, it'll help you sleep a lot better at night as well.

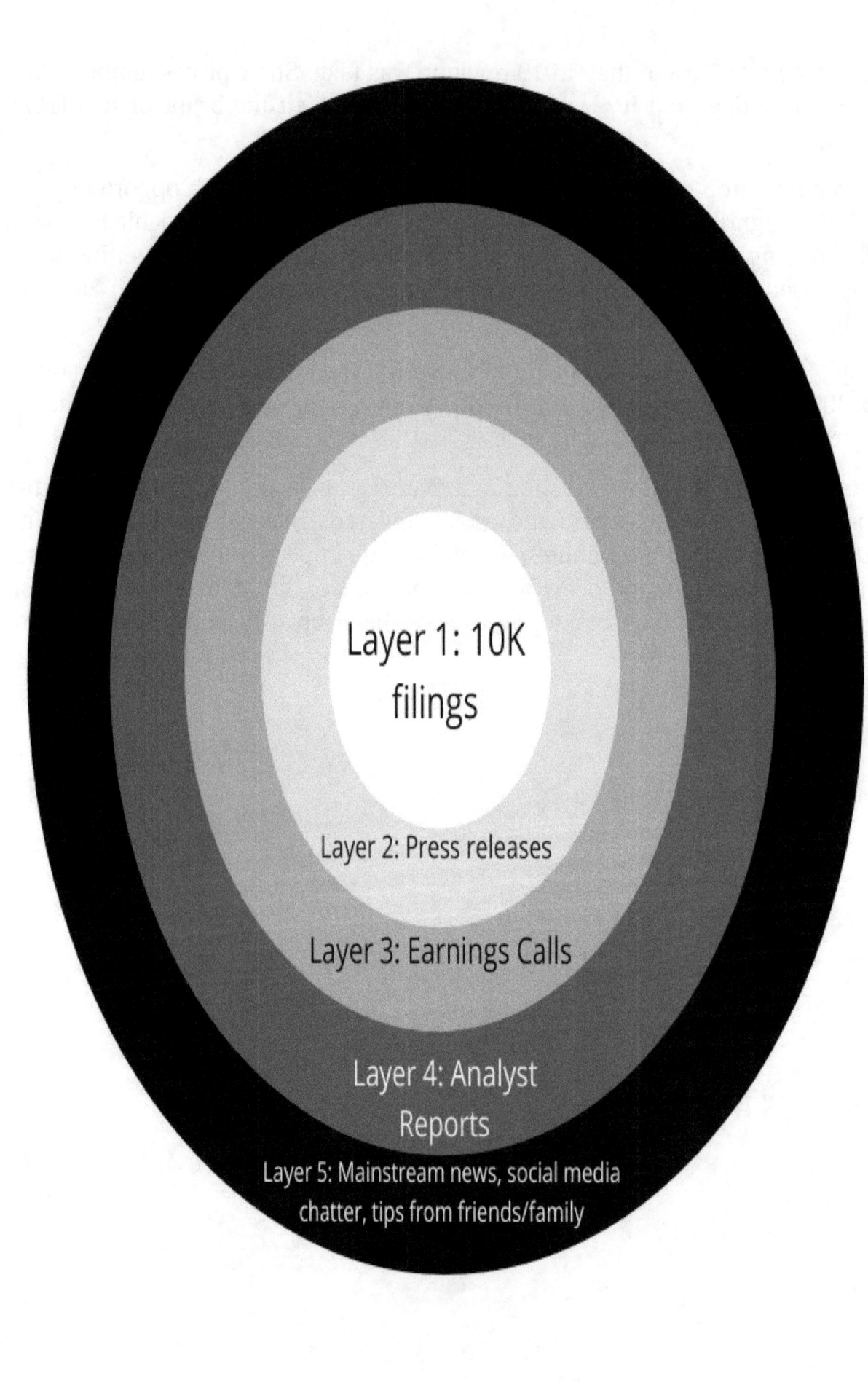

The Onion Model: Most investors start from the outside in, and never get past layer 5 before making their decision. The best investors start from the inside out, and make a decision before even acknowledging layer 5.

"ONCE WE REALIZE THAT IMPERFECT UNDERSTANDING IS THE HUMAN CONDITION THERE IS NO SHAME IN BEING WRONG, ONLY IN FAILING TO CORRECT OUR MISTAKES,"

George Soros, who made over $1 Billion in a single day in 1992 after shorting the British Pound during the UK's attempt to withdraw from the European Exchange Rate Mechanism.

4
NAVIGATING THE FLAWS IN HUMAN PSYCHOLOGY

You learned about how the confirmation bias skews your ability to properly analyze an opportunity. The fact is that human beings are subject to a wide range of biases that cloud our ability to judge situations. These flaws are deep-seated evolutionary instincts and it's close to impossible to get rid of them. In fact, you might not even want to do this.

The good news is that you can become aware of them and choose to ignore their call in a given situation. Money and investing is an intensely emotional process. In order to be successful at it, you have to keep these biases in mind and guard against them. Making money over the long term often boils down to avoiding mental traps as opposed to coming up with a genius-level plan.

This chapter is going to introduce you to some of the most common flaws in human thinking and show you how you can navigate them.

THE BLOOD IN THE STREETS PROBLEM

"Be fearful when others are greedy and be greedy when others are fearful."

Out of the thousands of Warren Buffett quotes regularly touted by the media, this one, more than any other, has received the most airtime lately. Like many of his statements, there is a lot of nuance to it that is often lost on the wider public. Even investors who study his methods fall prey to this kind of thinking.

They assume a default position of looking to buy stocks the minute the market begins to fall. They wear contrarian badges proudly and neglect to realize that they're being overly greedy in this scenario and aren't investing intelligently.

Buffett's statement is a good philosophy to adopt, but it isn't something that should be applied at every turn. Not every low-priced stock is a good buy and not every high-priced stock is a potential sell. You still need to do the work and analyze what's going on underneath.

Believing in this philosophy blindly will cause you to fall victim to your confirmation bias. You'll spot a low-priced stock and automatically believe that it's a great opportunity. Your analysis will now be colored by this thought and you'll filter out information that proves the opposite case.

The best way to guard against these situations is to use Charlie Munger's advice and recognize that truly outstanding opportunities occur very rarely in life. The majority of the opportunities you receive are going to be below par. As a result, even if you miss them, you're not going to lose out too much. The important stuff has a way of finding you, and you'll be able to recognize it when it comes.

The partnership of Buffett and Munger has worked well for the both of them. Why not use their philosophies to form a partnership in your mind to help you as well?

Another behavior that often occurs by believing Buffett's philosophy to an extreme is when investors become obsessed with calling the bottom of the bear market. They're impatient to enter the market and as a result, begin thinking of every bottom as the moment when prices are about to swing the other way.

This only results in them investing in short rallies. The market drops ever lower and they keep losing money by exiting and reentering even lower.

Stay away from this kind of behavior if you wish to make long term profits. Instead, evaluate every situation on its own merit and be aware of your propensity to believe in this philosophy a little too much.

LEARNING TO APPRECIATE A CRISIS

We've touched upon this sentiment previously. Bear markets offer investors a huge opportunity to enter some of the best companies in the market at bargain basement prices. Crises often inject a lot of emotion into the markets and people overreact to such announcements.

For example, the COVID-19 pandemic will have a significant impact on businesses. However, the extent of the initial fall in the markets was grossly exaggerated. There were some truly excellent companies that were available at 20-25% discounts from their true value. Many of them were companies we already held such as Starbucks, Berkshire Hathaway and McDonald's. Needless to say, we loaded up on them to lower our cost basis.

The reasoning behind buying even more of these companies wasn't that their prices had dropped. It was that their underlying economics hadn't changed. These underlying factors were the reason for investing in them in the first place. As long as these remained intact, the only logical thing to do was to buy more of them.

If you can act rationally while the markets are irrational, you'll make a lot of money. This is why a crisis offers a huge opportunity for the intelligent investor. Emotions run riot during these times and inefficiencies pile up to create huge discounts between price and value.

STOP CHASING MOMENTUM

During bull markets, buying high-momentum stocks is a popular strategy. The stocks that have historically exhibited higher growth levels than the broader market typically rise a lot quicker when times are good. Many momentum investors bring this philosophy to bear markets as well.

They reason that if stocks that rise higher than the market provide gains in bull markets, stocks that fall faster than the rest will make them money in bear markets. This sounds great on paper, but unfortunately it doesn't work this way. Shorting everything in sight isn't a strategy. Shorting refers to when an investor can sell a stock first before buying it back for a lower price.

Bear markets usually witness lower participation from people. This is because no one likes it when markets go down and the average investor is uncomfortable with the shorting process. Bull markets witness huge levels of involvement and as a result, pretty much every stock tends to rise. You can get away with buying everything in sight because there are large numbers of other investors who are doing the same thing.

Due to volumes being lower in bear markets, this effect doesn't carry over. To modify what Tolstoy once wrote, all stocks rise for the same reasons, but every stock declines for different reasons. Some might drop in an unjustified manner while some will drop for fully valid reasons.

You'll need to examine them individually to determine what the reason for the drop is. Assuming that bear market irrationality carries over to each and every individual company is the wrong thing to do.

Then there's the other side of the coin. Some investors believe that once the market has fallen low enough, every stock in it is a worthwhile buy. This is just as much of an error as shorting everything is. They feel that since everything that has fallen must rise at some point, every company is a reasonable buy.

There are investors out there who are still buying companies such as Luckin Coffee, airlines and cruise ship operators just because their prices have dropped a lot. In Luckin's case, the drop was caused by financial fraud. In the case of airlines and cruise ship operators, it's still unknown how they'll recover from the restrictions imposed by the pandemic.

Companies go bankrupt all the time. The good times lead investors to forget this crucial fact. They forget that businesses will face tough conditions at some point in the road. The ones that prepare for them beforehand are the ones that survive. The ones that load themselves up with leverage tend to be exposed when the music stops.

Perhaps the most egregious example in the current market is that of Hertz. Retail investors were buying up huge amounts of stock, even after the company declared Chapter 11 Bankruptcy. In a 6 day period in March 2020, the stock price went from $3.38 to $8.21. An increase of 148.04%. A similar trend occurred in June 2020 when the price went from $1.50 to $5.53, an increase of 268.67%.

Most alarmingly of all, these trends continued after Hertz issued $500 million in new shares. The share release prospectus (an SEC mandated 8-K filing) including the word "worthless", alluding to future stock values, a staggering 7 times. For day traders, these wild fluctuations in share price might be a positive. But for long-term investors, we can't think of a worse company to buy right now than one currently going through bankruptcy procedures, and facing a delisting from the New York Stock Exchange.

Just because stocks are cheap, does not make them a worthwhile investment.

Stocks can and do go to zero.

So stop chasing trends in bear markets. Whether the trends are up or down, don't buy or sell stocks just because the strategy worked in a bull market. This is how you'll lose money.

DON'T OVERREACT TO NEWS

Bear markets cause most market participants to lose their heads. They see doomsday warnings everywhere and this causes huge price movements in the markets. This is referred to as volatility. Volatility is a measure of how fast and how far a particular instrument in the market moves.

Bull markets witness volatility but of a different kind. Due to the abundance of good news and due to everyone jumping into the market believing it's going higher, the market moves quickly in one direction (upwards.)

Bear markets experience a different kind of volatility. Due to uncertainty and fear pervading the markets, prices jump up and down to a huge degree all the time. This results in a lot of investors getting cleaned out. Take for instance the shenanigans that surrounded the price of oil recently.

Due to lockdowns being imposed, the demand for oil crashed to lows. As a result, the price of oil moved into negative territory for the first time ever. Oil is traded through futures contracts. These contracts are valid for a month and anyone who buys them is effectively locking in a purchase of oil for that month.

Prices moving into negative territory was a quirk of the futures market. Physical oil was still selling at positive prices. However, a few investors reasoned that the quirk of pricing in the market could be exploited. There were a number of news outlets that jumped on the hysteria as well and screamed that "oil was negative!" and so on.

A large number of investors bought oil-related instruments in the hope of witnessing a positive jump. However, they underestimated the degree to which they understood the oil market. As a result, they ended up getting cleaned out. It wasn't the bear market that caused them a loss. It was their lack of understanding of the instrument they were investing in.

This lack of understanding came about because they'd put their blinders on and were convinced they'd spotted an opportunity. They treated it as the deal of a lifetime. If they'd instead followed Charlie Munger's advice as highlighted before, they'd have been able to get rid of their confirmation bias and would have stepped aside.

There are a lot of market participants out there who have no idea what they're talking about. In this age of social media, you're going to be bombarded with all of their opinions and they'll likely sound very convincing and smart. Of course, they'll still be wrong for the most part.

Going bargain hunting in sectors or assets you do not understand is the easiest way for you to lose money. We'll cover this in more detail shortly. The COVID-19 pandemic is already witnessing a raft of intelligent-sounding social media discussions and media coverage when it comes to companies in the pharmaceutical sector.

Almost every drug maker is now working on a potential cure that is extremely promising. The expected bump upwards in share prices duly arrives shortly after such announcements. Popular themes tend to be used in this way by companies to boost their share prices.

The best example of this is a small beverage maker based out of Long Island, NY. The company's name was Long Island Iced Tea after the famous adult beverage. Despite the name, it sold iced teas with a small degree of success. However, in 2017 it announced that it would change its name to Long Blockchain corp and would begin to explore opportunities in blockchain technology (Cheng, 2017). Which sounds like a perfectly reasonable thing for a beverage maker to do.

Shares of Long Island Iced Tea duly jumped over 200% and eventually settled at 183% above the opening price before the announcement. There was no reason for this jump other than the word "blockchain" being added to the name. No one stopped to question why on earth a reasonably successful beverage maker was switching its focus to blockchain.

Instead, its share price rose thanks to the millions of uninformed investors thinking this was a bargain of a lifetime and the chance to get in on something great. Needless to say these shenanigans got the company into trouble and it was eventually investigated by the SEC.

STOP HUNTING FOR SHORT-TERM SUCCESS STORIES

As human beings, we love believing in optimistic happy endings. Even the most hardcore pessimists among us love to believe that things will turn out fine in the end. While this applies to the big picture, it doesn't necessarily apply to every single entity within that picture.

For example, the market might recover well in the long run, but there's no guarantee that all of the current companies in the market will recover along with it. Most investors don't extend their thinking beyond the most obvious of consequences that a company might be facing.

This illustrates the importance of second order thinking. This is in contrast to first order thinking. For example, if you're hungry and someone gives you a bar of chocolate, you reason that the chocolate will satisfy you. Hence, you arrive at the conclusion that eating the bar of chocolate is good for you. This is first order thinking.

Second order thinking requires you to go a bit further and ask "then what?" Once you've eaten the chocolate, then what happens? You'll feel full, but is this really the best option for your health? Will it cause you harm thanks to all of the other chocolate bars you've eaten? Thinking in this way will get you to reason that a healthier snack might be in order.

The right decision often comes from engaging in second order thinking. This is especially true when the first order choice is negative or distasteful. You might not feel like waking up in the morning and exercising because you slept late last night. However, if you keep sleeping in, you'll not hit your fitness goals and this will cause even bigger problems down the road.

When it comes to investing, first order thinking is prevalent everywhere. This is what causes the stock price of companies like Zoom and Netflix to rocket upwards. At one point Zoom was selling at a PE ratio of 1000! This is more than sixty times the price of comparable companies in its sector.

The reasoning behind such a large price rise is due to evaluating first order consequences. People are going to be confined to their homes a lot more and will therefore use both apps increasingly. However, what are the second order consequences of being at home for longer?

Is Zoom capable of cashing in on its newfound fame? It is an app designed primarily for B2B communication. It has already faced a crisis when users discovered security flaws within its structure. While the company has dealt with this admirably, is there some other danger that Zoom is exposed to because of this new army of users?

Then there's Netflix. The company has witnessed higher user numbers. However, it's producing original content at a much faster rate and is investing the same amount of money into creating it as Disney currently is. Disney has revenue streams and valuable trademarks to backup its investment.

Netflix has nowhere near this kind of cushion. Can it sustain profits despite investing this much into content creation?

Often, the worst consequences come from decisions that have positive first order effects and negative second and even third order effects. For example, let's say a new CFO joins a startup and, in a bid to make a great impression, decides to do away with free snacks and meals.

The first order effect is huge cost savings for the company and a boost to its bottom line. The second order effect is older employees getting disillusioned and jumping ship because things aren't the same. The employees who joined the startup are who made the company what it is, so this will leave a mark.

A third order effect might be the startup's competition realizing the importance of free snacks and they might begin offering this to their employees. As a result, talented employees jump ship to the competition and the startup struggles to attract talent, let alone grow.

Short-term success stories are typically the result of first order thinking. Believing that everything will be fine and that things will go back to the way they once were only causes you to look for positive first order consequences. For example, with the pandemic having enforced a new normal in people's lives, everyone wants to go back to the time when things weren't this way.

However as the pandemic has proven, the world was extremely fragile in 2019. Is this really a state we want to spend our lives in? In a world that is on the verge of being turned upside down without adequate support? Where excess leverage is rewarded and where economic prosperity is just an illusion?

Considering second order effects gets you thinking in this manner, and in the markets it will make you money. An added bonus is that you'll have less competition to deal with!

EVALUATING YOUR CURRENT PORTFOLIO

Bear markets bring significant shocks to the system and your portfolio is going to feel these effects. Before making a move to get rid of any of your current holdings, ask yourself if the underlying economics of the business has changed. Have any of your original investment considerations changed at all

If the answer is yes, then you should exit your investment. However, if there hasn't been any change in the underlying business, you should be buying more. If the business was a good buy at $50, it must be an even better buy at $30.

By forcing yourself to look at the underlying business in a logical manner, you'll end up acting in rational terms. You will stick to your original investment thesis and avoid haphazardly jumping in and out of stocks.

If price shocks really bother you and if you're looking to lock in your unrealized profit, you can use what is called a trailing stop loss order. A stop loss order protects your downside risk on your investment. This is a sell order that you place with your broker and instructs them to sell your investment if the market dips below a certain price.

For example, if you buy a stock at $100 and place a stop loss at $80, your maximum loss on this order is $20. Now if the stock moves up to $120, you've earned an unrealized paper profit of $20. If you would like to lock in some profit, you could place a trailing stop loss order that is $10 away from the current market price thereby locking in 50% of the price rise.

As the stock price keeps rising, your stop loss order keeps rising with it and "trails" the market price. This allows you to lock in whatever profit you've made. If the market moves back down too swiftly, you'll exit your investment at the trailing stop loss level and will keep your gains.

DON'T WATCH WHAT PEOPLE SAY—WATCH WHAT THEY DO

Many investors turn to the mainstream financial press and their favorite blogs during bearish times in search of guidance. This isn't a bad thing by itself. After all, you do need to remain up to date with what's going on in the markets. The problem occurs when you begin to use these sources as justifications for investment actions.

Thanks to the media's obsession with finding a bottom for the bear market, you'll hear statements from hedge fund managers proclaiming that they're now bullish. A few others will come out and say that they're bearish. Eventually these two opposing parties will be brought on air to argue against one another.

At the end of the day nothing gets decided and the market does whatever it wants to do. A lot of these arguments are set up by the media and these hedge fund managers often don't believe the things they proclaim. The best way to figure out where someone stands is to look at what they do, instead of listening to what they say.

If an investor is bullish, have they been buying anything? What does their portfolio look like? If the investor doesn't offer proof for their statements, there's no need to listen to them. Examine their statements for consistency as well.

One website that offers a look at the portfolios of famous investors is gurufocus.com. On the site you can see the current portfolios of investors like Warren Buffett, Carl Icahn and Bill Ackman, as well as other businessmen like Bill Gates. For example, did you know almost 10% of Bill Gates' portfolio is in utilities company Waste Management (NYSE:WM)?

Opinions change all the time. However, you can't invest on the basis of someone changing their opinion every other day.

In fact, take everyone else's opinion with a large grain of salt. You don't know what their motivations are and where they're coming from. Evaluate their words objectively, watch what they do and see if those actions make sense for you. If they don't, feel free to ignore them.

YOUR STOCK DOESN'T LOVE YOU

Or perhaps we should say, your stock doesn't love you as much as you love your stock. You cannot hold onto your investments just because you've developed an emotional bond with them. Many investors become attached to their holdings and fall right into the trap of the sunken cost fallacy.

This is an emotional bias that we develop. If you've invested money into something, you're now deeply affected by its prospects. If it declines, you think that you'll simply ride out the bottom of the curve and wait until it gets back to where it was. Besides, pulling the trigger and cutting the investment loose will cause you to lose money.

That's painful for a lot of investors. As we mentioned earlier, you need to objectively evaluate your reasons for investment and check if they're still valid. If the underlying business has changed, you need to let go of your investments and cut your losses (if any) as quickly as possible.

You know you're a rational investor when you have the confidence to short the very stocks you once bought!

AVOID NARRATIVE INVESTING

Every one of us loves a good story. Unfortunately, successful investing doesn't care much for your stories. It relies on facts and logic. If a company isn't successfully hitting its targets with its product, that company is going to decline. If it doesn't follow good business principles, it's going to decline.

This example is a bit old, but it's worth pointing out. Concorde was and still remains the only fully functioning supersonic commercial airplane. It was developed in 1969 and was an engineering marvel. Calling it an engineering marvel is an understatement in fact ("When Did Concorde First Fly to North America?," 2020).

The plane was never significantly updated in terms of technology until its retirement in 2003. Despite this, it was still faster than any modern commercial airliner. Concorde could fly from London to New York in an average time of three and a half hours, with the fastest flight time coming in just under three hours.

Modern airplanes cover the same distance in just under eight hours. The plane had an average cruising altitude of 65,000 feet. This meant passengers could look at space up above if they peeked outside their windows. They could see the curvature of the earth as well. Concorde wasn't a plane as much as it was an experience.

It was also a monumental flop, as such things sadly are. Despite the wonderful experience every passenger had, the plane was commercially unsuccessful. British Airways and Air France never earned a profit on Concorde flights. The plane was fuel-efficient at supersonic speed. However, getting there meant it had to accelerate to Mach Two over populated areas.

This meant that all houses over Concorde's flight path were subject to sonic booms. European governments soon outlawed mainland continental Concorde flights due to this. Not that it mattered anyway. Concorde needed long flight distances to truly stretch its legs and New York to London was the only route at the time that had sufficient demand.

A tragic accident in Paris in 2000 that involved an Air France Concorde, but was not caused by any faults in the plane, sealed its reputation in France. It never flew from France again. British Airways struggled with it until finally pulling the plug in 2003. A marvelous engineering feat that showed what humanity was capable of was put out of action with little ceremony.

As emotional as people became over Concorde, there's no denying that it was never going to succeed and it didn't make sense to invest in it (assuming you had the chance.) People get emotional about the products their portfolio companies make as well.

You can invest in a company that is making a product that is going to change the world. However, if this product isn't going to be commercially successful, that company is going nowhere. Investors form such world-changing narratives in their minds and this causes them to ignore facts. Concorde should have been put out of its misery in the 1980s, but sheer emotion kept the flights operational. British Airways and Air France had their confirmation bias blinders on fully and only looked at the positives.

One of the worst mistakes you can make as an investor is to retrofit your emotional investment thesis to sound rational. For example, you might like the way Tesla's cars look and believe in Elon Musk's drive and energy. You might also believe that electric cars are going to take over the world. You thus decide to invest in Tesla stock without looking at the numbers and underlying business.

When someone asks you why you invested in Tesla you then say something about how Musk is disrupting thought and how Tesla is disrupting the automotive sector and the internal combustion engine and so on. By doing this you've given your emotional decision the veneer of logic.

Our point is not to say that Tesla is a bad investment. It's to say that you need to be careful and avoid falling into narrative traps such as these that aren't backed by facts. During bull markets, the majority of companies rise in value thanks to the overall mood of optimism. This means narrative investing works very well in such times. However, it falls apart in bear markets.

KNOWING YOUR CIRCLE OF COMPETENCE AND AVOIDING TOURIST TRAPS

A tourist trap is a stock that draws investment into itself purely because of headlines that highlight how cheap it is (Summers, 2020). Oil ETFs were a tourist trap recently thanks to the price of oil dipping below zero.

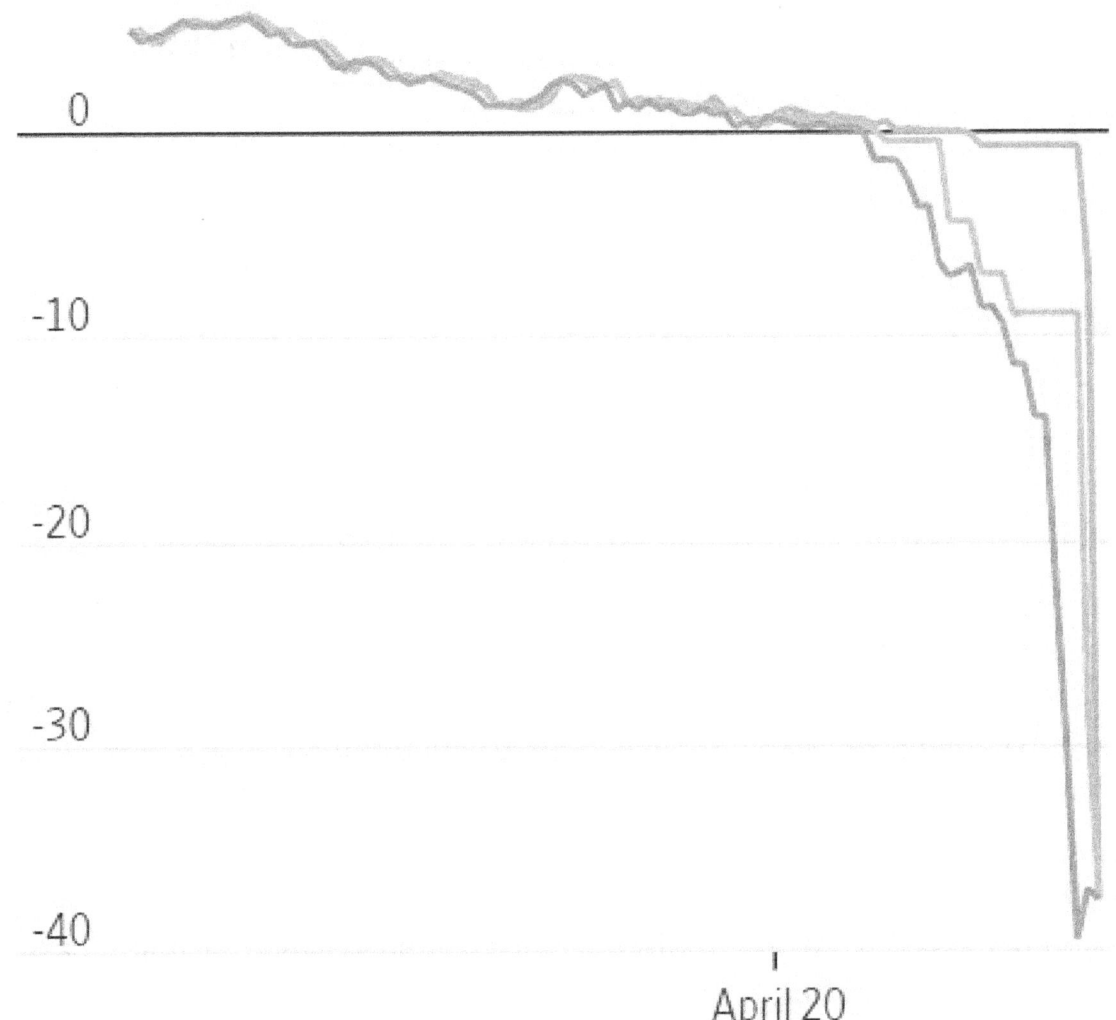

We've already highlighted the example of investors who poured their money into buying oil-related instruments and were burned by the market. This occurred due to them straying away from their circle of competence. The circle of competence is a fancy term for explaining all of the things you know well.

For example, a medical doctor's circle of competence extends to their field and practice. It probably does not include knowledge on how to build a rocket. An NFL athlete's circle of competence extends to his sport. He might be above average at another sport, like baseball, but it's no guarantee that he'll be elite at it or be able to play professionally.

In real life, most people stay away from things that call for specialized expertise. If a pipe bursts, you call a plumber. However, put someone in front of a trading screen and suddenly they're experts at evaluating everything from a utilities company to a technology company.

This behavior gets really bad when people begin investing in certain exchange traded funds (ETFs). ETFs are a great, low-cost way to invest, but a lot of the market surrounding them has misled people. They are convenient, but ETFs are effectively hedge funds for the everyday investor. Each fund has a particular strategy that the fund manager follows. There are simple ETFs such as SPY that track the broad stock market by owning all of the stocks in the S&P 500.

However, the common misconception is that ETFs work this way. Many ETFs do not own the underlying asset. This is the case for many ETFs which retail investors buy to get exposure to non-equity markets like commodities or precious metals. For example, the USO ETF attempts to mimic the price of oil by trading oil futures. Investing in futures contracts means that the fund has to utilize leverage (borrow money).

Once the oil market went into meltdown, this put USO in a very bad situation. Its assets were deteriorating and its creditors were turning up asking for their money. So with oil prices hovering near zero, many traders felt that USO would be a good buy. What these traders didn't realize is that because they were trading in futures contracts and not the spot price of oil, prices could go negative. This happens as the fund itself would have to pay others to take the futures contracts off their hands. This is exactly what happened, as prices crashed to -$37.63. However for many retails investors, their investment platform showed positive prices on the screen, likely due to the way the software had been programmed. It wasn't until the following day when they realized that they had suffered catastrophic losses.

This was because USO practiced what is called a next month rollover. A rollover happens when an investor shifts their position from the current month futures contract to the contract that expires one month after that. USO had religiously rolled its contracts over every month for the last 10 years when the current month futures expired.

With the current month price near 0 and the next month's price at $12, investors figured they could capture that huge price swing. All they had to do was buy USO and wait for the rollover.

Except the rollover never came. USO announced it would be restructuring its contracts and that the rollover was being modified. This meant that all investors who had bet on the rollover lost their shirts. Was this legal? Yes. This was the point that these investors missed. USO was not bound to rollover their contacts in the first place! It was entirely up to management to do so. Professional firms knew this and profited handsomely, but it was retail investors who paid the price. According to the Wall Street Journal, Interactive Brokers had to pay more than $100m to cover for traders whose "holdings" ended up in the negative.

These investors' losses were caused by not understanding what they were investing in. as well as playing in areas that were well beyond their circle of competence. When investing in ETFs, especially ones which are non-equity focused, don't let greed cloud your judgment. Always read the prospectus from the fund's website before buying and understand how it functions before putting money into it. If you find that you can't understand how the ETF works and what the investment strategy is, stay away from it.

"IF YOU FIND YOURSELF LOSING SLEEP OVER YOUR INVESTMENTS, SELL DOWN TO THE SLEEPING POINT"

Jesse Livermore, often referred to as the "Father of Day Trading"

HOW TO CAPITALIZE EFFECTIVELY IN A BEAR MARKET

You've learned that bear markets offer huge opportunities for the intelligent investor. How are you supposed to take advantage of them exactly? Every investor could do with a primer of sorts before we get into the details of bear market investment, and this is what you'll learn now.

These points are a mix of tips and best practices for bear markets. They'll help you prepare for those times and will also keep you safe.

OPTIMIZE YOUR ACTIVITY LEVELS

How active should you be in a bear market? Given that there will be more opportunities for you to invest in, it stands to reason that you'll be more active in bear markets than in bullish ones. However, being active merely for the sake of it doesn't make any sense.

Some investors understand that bear markets offer huge opportunities but get carried away with the thought of finding them. This causes them to put their confirmation bias blinders on, and they soon find themselves buying into investment ideas that have no merit.

It's important for you to always keep the basic principles of investment in mind. Just because a market has turned bearish, this doesn't mean you're obliged to find opportunities. Some investors might have their egos hurt and think they're missing out on huge opportunities.

They might begin to question their analysis process and think they're being far too conservative. They might end up modifying or loosening their criteria, and the next thing you know, they're buying the likes of Luckin Coffee because they cannot think of anything else to buy.

Remember that there's no rule saying that you have to invest in a bear market. Whether bullish or bearish, the principles of sound investment are the same. You need to evaluate companies within your circle of competence and you need to understand what their business is all about.

If you cannot understand something, you need to stay away from it. This applies to all forms of investment, by the way, and all asset classes as well. A good example to highlight here is the case of Warren Buffett. He famously avoided technology stocks for the majority of his career.

Even after the dotcom crash in 2000, he stayed away from investing in technology companies despite the presence of some huge bargains. He could have theoretically bought Apple, Microsoft, Amazon and Intel for pennies on the dollar in terms of their true worth.

What's more, this wasn't the first time Buffett passed on Intel. The founder of Intel, Bob Noyce, approached Buffett for startup capital after being introduced by a mutual friend. Buffett passed on the offer because he didn't understand the business or its economics (Schroeder, 2008).

Ordinary investors who get burned in bear markets routinely think and fantasize that they could have bought this or that for cheap when the market crashed. They don't pay attention to their circle of competence and get carried away with make-believe numbers they could have earned as a return.

These investors mistake activity with productivity. It's a lot like the office worker who is constantly busy but gets nothing done on time. The issue isn't with their energy levels. It's the efficiency and method of working that's the problem. As an investor, your job is to look at and source opportunities that fit your style of investing.

Your style is defined by your philosophy about the markets. If you happen to understand one particular sector better than others, then dive deeply into it. If you happen to understand the casino business very well and can reasonably predict what might occur next, then find the best casino stocks to invest in.

Don't go around chasing biotech stocks because someone told you they're the future. Or 5G stocks or any such companies whose business you don't understand.

Another mistake that investors make when the market begins to decline is to look at small cap stocks exclusively in the hopes of unearthing bargains. Small cap stocks refer to companies that are between $300 million to $2 billion in size. These stocks have potential for greater returns than large cap stocks, but they're also extremely risky. After all, these are tiny companies and they face a lot of obstacles. The investor chasing them reasons that in bear markets not only will good small cap companies decline in price, they'll also have a large runway to grow.

This means the investor can earn huge returns. By doing this, the investor is trying to find the next Amazon or next Google. Typically, such investments go nowhere. Instead of beginning in this manner, start with what you know and work forward from there.

If your circle of competence happens to include a small cap company, then go ahead and analyze it further. Don't feel compelled to invest money into a company just because you feel you need to be doing something in a bear market.

PREPARE FOR DIPS

Remember what Keynes said about markets? About how they can be irrational for a lot longer than the investor expects? Well, this is going to affect your portfolio. The average bear market investor can expect the value of their portfolio to almost certainly decline in the short term.

This is because very few people manage to invest at the exact moment when the market turns back up after hitting their lowest low. There's a saying in investment circles that bear markets test your stomach more than your brains. You need to mentally prepare yourself to watch your investment sink in value.

This can be difficult because potential loss affects us more than potential gain. Cognitive Psychologist Daniel Kahneman first brought this idea to the stock market sphere in his seminal work *Thinking Fast and Slow*. Kahneman explains that this loss aversion is why we tend to act more based on perceived losses (panic selling stock), than we do after perceived gains (buying more).

There will also be the onslaught of television and social media constantly telling you how investors "lost" one billion or one trillion or whatever number they come up with. You need to understand that these "losses" they're talking about are all on paper. If you bought a share of stock at $100 and watched it decline to $50 and have still not sold it, you've not lost anything.

You'll realize the loss only when you sell it. The same applies to when markets rise. If your investment rises to $200, you've not gained anything anywhere, other than on paper. You realize gains and losses only when you sell. If the underlying business is great and if you continue to hold onto the investment, you'll see the price rise back up at some point.

A good analogy that explains market movements was provided by Benjamin Graham. He created a fictional character called Mr. Market. Mr. Market was quite a character. Some days, he'd offer you $100 for your stock, which was right about what it was worth. On other days, he'd get depressed and offer you $20 for it. On some other days he'd suffer from a dose of euphoria and would offer you $300 for it. There was no rhyme or reason to what Mr. Market would do. All you had to do was receive his offer and decide whether you wanted to take him up on it.

This analogy doubly applies to bear markets. On some days you'll find that your stock has been in a rally and it's up by a large amount. Everyone will be cheering about the end of the bear market. You might even be looking forward to seeing green in your portfolio after a long time.

However, as with most bear market rallies, it will end and you're going to be staring at red again for a while. During these moments, it's best to remind yourself that all of these movements are just on paper. They're not real unless you decide to sell.

To clarify, we're not recommending you keep holding onto an investment in the hopes that it will rise. The point is to analyze every investment in your portfolio objectively and figure out which ones are still good businesses. You must hold onto or add to only such investments. The rest should be sold immediately.

A good way to prepare for such moments is to simply not check the prices of your investments. Focus only on following the relevant news surrounding your businesses and keep track of news releases and legal filings. The 10-Qs might not be the most reliable, but it will give you something to focus on in between 10-K filings.

If you have capital to invest, you should also be looking for further investment bargains.

MAINTAIN HEALTHY CASH RESERVES

If you're going to take advantage of mispriced assets in the market you'll need to have cash on hand to invest. When setting aside cash to invest, it's extremely important for you to plan well in advance. For starters you should not be investing cash that you'll need anytime soon.

This rules out any emergency money that you need for your living expenses, money for your kid's college tuition, money that needs to be put towards a down payment and so on. You need to invest money that you will not be needing for a long time in the future, for the next 10 years at the very least.

The first reason for this is any investment carries a certain degree of risk. You don't want to be risking money you need to survive. If you end up losing 50% or even more of your capital and this money was meant to pay the bills, you can imagine the chaos that would ensue in your life.

The second reason is that stock market investments need time to flourish. When speaking of bear markets, no one knows how long they'll last. They might last for two years, or they might last for five. Your investment needs time to grow because companies don't turn into behemoths overnight.

By remaining invested for a long time, you're also giving yourself the best chance of compounding your investment. Compounding refers to your money earning a steady interest rate over time. For example, if you invest $1,000 into a company that rises by 10% every year for 10 years, you'll have $2,593 at the end of this time. That's a 159.3% return despite the sum of the yearly interest adding up to 100% (10% multiplied by 10 years).

Compounding allows you to earn an additional 59.3% of your principal for free. The catch is, you can't touch the sum and need to remain invested. The best part about compounding is that your overall return increases the longer you remain invested. In 20 years your $1,000 would have grown to $6,727. That's a 572.7% return despite the sum of yearly interest adding up to 200%. You've earned an additional 372.7% return for free!

The method is very much like a snowball. It begins with little additions, but as it starts rolling downhill and collecting more and more momentum, its size increases. Soon, you've started an avalanche.

Something that can accelerate your returns is leverage. Brokers offer margin accounts that allow you to borrow money to buy stocks. You might be tempted to follow the example of Sir John Templeton and borrow money to buy shares in companies you like. Unless you are already very experienced, do not do this.

Bear markets tend to fall a lot faster than bull markets rise. This means you'll have less time to figure out what's going on and when things go bad, they'll go bad quick. You'll be hit with a margin call, which is when a broker asks you to deposit more money to cover your losses, and risk being cleaned out.

It doesn't matter how attractive the price is or how sure a shot you believe the opportunity is. You need to cover your bottom-line risk first. While Templeton made his money by using leverage, there have been plenty of other investors who haven't needed its power to earn huge returns. If they didn't need it, you don't either.

Plenty of investors focus far too much on the rewards on offer and don't think about the risks they run while investing. The stock market is a risky place and companies go bust all the time. Especially in bear markets. It is possible for you to make a mistake and lose your investment.

Instead of trying to hit home runs all the time, try to avoid poor decisions. Limit your risks and only invest what you can afford. The ultimate test of successful investment is whether you can sleep at night.

PLAY EARNINGS SEASON CORRECTLY

For the average investor, planning purchases around earnings season is usually not a great idea. Stocks during this time will experience high volatility and they'll be subject to the market's perceived first order risks. For example, some investors think that a company might not meet its earnings expectations and they'll plan on buying it at lower prices around earnings announcements.

To their dismay, they might find that not only does the stock price remain stable, it rises. This might be because the company's earnings aren't as bad as everyone thought they might be. The reasons for your entry should never depend on capturing a price around earnings seasons.

If your investment is going to be that price-sensitive, you're probably looking at too short a time horizon for your investment and are speculating on the price. For example, if you plan on buying a stock at $100 and holding it for just a month, it's unlikely to move far beyond $110 or $90 in that time. These are 10% movements, and most stocks don't move that much even in volatile markets.

Should your purchase price be $105, this reduces your potential profit quite a bit. However, if you were planning on holding this stock for 10 years, the potential ceiling for the price is unlimited. Who knows how far it could rise? If someone told you that the price of this stock would be $500 in 10 years' time, would you care about $100 versus $105?

Chances are that you won't. You should care about price in relation to value. When buying a stock, you need to have a good margin of safety built into the purchase price. A margin of safety is simply a buffer you build for yourself against adverse price movement.

For example, when you prepare a budget for yourself, you probably add a "Miscellaneous" line in there to account for unexpected expenses. This is the margin of safety or buffer you've given yourself. Similarly, if you determine the fair value of a stock to be $110, you want to buy it at a fair discount so that, even if you're wrong, you still have some room for yourself.

The exact amount of the margin of safety depends on your temperament as an investor. Whatever this might be, if you're worrying about a dollar here or there, you're probably not building a big enough buffer for yourself. For example, if your safety margin is 20%, you'll look to pay around $88. If you end up buying at $90 or even $95, you've still got yourself a good deal.

The problem starts arising when you're buying at $105 or $108. You're pretty close to fair value and as a result, you're far more price-sensitive.

Coming back to earnings season, stocks will have their first order consequences factored into their price. As a result, you won't witness huge levels of volatility unless something unexpected happens. Stay away from trying to time your entries according to earnings expectations.

If a company's business is solid and if you're not price-sensitive, then how does a difference of a few dollars on entry matter to your investment? In percentage terms, it's going to be a very small portion of your projected gain. Be aware of earnings but don't use them to time entries.

EXAMINE YOURSELF: HOW ARE YOU WRONG?

Charles Darwin had an interesting mental approach when it came to publishing his work. His method was quite simple at first glance (Parrish, 2020). After he was done postulating a theory for publishing, he would go for a walk. On this walk, he would contemplate all the ways in which he was wrong and why his theory was false.

He would conduct a debate within his mind and would fervently argue for the opposite side, trying to poke holes in his own theory. This approach is something that many successful people have adopted, from Charlie Munger to Reed Hastings, the CEO of Netflix.

Hastings in fact encourages his staff to practice the method as well. When two managers within the company disagree with each other over a point, Hastings has them debate one another. The exception is that each person argues for the other side. This allows them to view all the holes in their own argument and brings more empathy to the process.

This simple thought process is quite difficult to practice in reality. We love our own ideas, and if they happen to be particularly insightful or contain even a morsel of insight, we jump on board and refuse to look at anything else. Confirmation bias kicks in and we rationalize everything else to fit our model.

The bias is so strong that even when we nominally sit down to consider the other side of the argument, we often focus on the negatives and ignore the positives. After this cursory process, we go right back to what we believe in. This sort of thinking favors no one.

Take the time to draw an argument for the other side. Poke holes relentlessly in your own theories. Remember Munger's advice about the majority of opportunities not being worth your time. When analyzing an investment opportunity, have it prove itself worthy of your time and attention.

This doesn't mean you set up barriers that are far too high to be breached. Instead, adopt an attitude of slight disinterest in your mind. Imagine that Mr. Market has brought you this proposal and you know how he behaves on a daily basis, with his constant drama and manic depressiveness.

Adopt this air of detachment and you're not going to get sucked into believing you're infallible. When you've formed your thesis fully, argue for the other side. The point isn't to launch ad hominem attacks at yourself. Instead, imagine that another person with your qualities is looking at this idea and it's your job to let them know why it might not work.

It's tough to do this objectively, but once you start doing it, you'll find that it's a foolproof method to verify and validate a lot of information you receive, not just investment related. If you find there's no compelling evidence against your idea, you know you're onto something good.

HOW TO HEDGE YOUR CURRENT PORTFOLIO

In our research for this book, we found that the majority of retail investors we spoke to had 2 things in common. Number 1, their portfolio was long only, which is to be expected during the conditions we experienced in the previous decade. The more alarmingly commonality was that 100% of their portfolio was in equities, so they were not holding bonds or precious metals. If they did have alternative investments, it was mostly in cryptocurrency.

This becomes an issue during bear markets as equities, especially in high-tech sectors tend to get crushed. For example, between October 2007 and February 2009, the S&P 500 fell by over 50%. Over the same time period, Gold was up over 50%, and 20-year treasury bonds were up 16%. Smart investors hedged their equity portfolios with precious metals and bonds, while the average retail investor saw their holdings get decimated.

So now that you have a good handle on the mental aspects of bear market investing and have gained a good idea of what you need to do before deploying your money in such investments, it's time to look at asset classes that tend to perform well in bear markets.

These asset classes are where you will have the most opportunity. Along the way, you're also going to learn all about some of the assets that don't do well during such times. You need to be aware of these assets because you'll likely find people jumping into them.

The media will also be touting them as being "hot," so it's imperative for you to understand why they won't provide you with good opportunities.

GOLD

There is a lot of debate surrounding gold and its value. Gold as a commodity doesn't offer any notable value to the economy or to any industrial process. Instead its value derives from the fact that everyone else thinks it is valuable. On the surface, it seems to be exactly the kind of investment asset that the intelligent investor ought to avoid. However, 5000 years of history give us a different perspective.

The primary argument for investing in gold is that it's a great hedge against inflation. The interesting thing about this argument is that it's incorrect over the short term but plays out quite well over the long term. For instance, a study conducted by professors at Duke University's Fuqua School of Business found that gold doesn't always work as an inflation hedge (Emspak, 2020).

That study also tried to determine the primary movers of gold prices but came up short. There's a good reason for this. Gold prices are moved mostly by fear. While intelligent investing should prioritize rationality, there's no doubt that human beings are emotional creatures. If there is an opportunity to capitalize on these emotions, it is irrational to ignore it.

Gold has risen in value over time (the past three decades) primarily due to huge levels of demand from India and China, where it is seen as a safe asset. One can understand this point of view. The people of those countries aren't that far removed from times where their currencies were devalued and the nation fell into default.

In India's case, the current working class demographic would have vivid memories of financial instability and times where the government was the only source of stable employment. China is more removed from highly unstable times, but the memories of those times don't fade away soon.

In short, gold is a very effective hedge against those local currencies, even if it doesn't always correlate to the relatively stable dollar and other Western currencies that have enjoyed generations of stability. Bear markets tend to increase fear in market participants and, as a result, gold always comes into the news.

However, it doesn't move when you would expect it to. Typically, gold spikes when the economy *exits* a downturn, not when it is entering one. The credit crisis proved this pattern during the previous decade. Gold witnessed a huge spike in 2008 but it managed to consistently rise and spiked to new highs throughout the bear market before peaking in 2011.

In fact, thanks to Quantitative Easing, and central banks printing money, the value of currency has declined. As a result, gold is seen as an asset that holds its value better.

This is because the more dollars a government prints, the less valuable its existing currency becomes. Gold on the other hand, cannot simply just be "printed" and yearly additions barely add to existing volumes.

There is a lot that doesn't make sense when it comes to gold, but given the way fear dominates in bear markets, these moments provide great opportunities for the intelligent investor. A research report from Bank of America projects that by October 2021, gold will likely hit a price of $3,000 per ounce (Wink, 2020). Others are even more bullish, with famed precious metals commentator Jim Rickards expecting long-term prices to hit $10,000 per ounce. This is due to the expected money printing that all central banks are expected to carry out to combat the downturn caused by the pandemic.

While $10,000 or even $3,000 per ounce might be a bit hyperbolic, there is no doubt that gold is expected to rise in value thanks to negative or close to zero interest rates present all around the world.

Due to these facts, and because of gold's historical utility in providing as a hedge against falling asset prices, we recommend all investors hold 10% of their portfolio in precious metals, with a priority given to gold holdings.

Ways To Invest in Gold

There are four major ways to invest in gold. These are:

1. Physical gold
2. ETFs which track the price of gold
3. Mining company stocks
4. Streamers

Physical gold, also called spot gold, allows the investor to touch and feel the gold they've bought. Some investors prefer the security that owning physical gold brings. After all, in case total economic collapse occurs, physical gold can still be used to trade for items. This might be an unlikely event, but it suits the mindset of certain investors.

There are many places you can buy physical gold from. The most obvious place is a jewelry shop, although in the West you're going to find a preponderance of diamonds in such stores. There are reliable online sources such as APMEX, J.M Bullion and wholesalecoindirect.com.

There are different kinds of spot gold you can purchase. Typically bullion is the most sought-after since this is pure gold, often 99.1% and above. Other forms of gold are usually alloyed with nickel or zinc to benefit certain industrial processes. The purest form of gold an investor can buy are Canadian Maple Leafs. These are 99.9% pure and are usually in the form of coins.

When buying physical gold, look for the name of the manufacturer, the purity and weight to be stamped on its face. Reputable mints include the Royal Canadian Mint, Valcambi and Perth Mint. The United States Mint also produces bars, but its major product happens to be coins.

Coins are a bit different from bars and aren't always the purest. Some coins, such as the US Mint American Eagle, are 91% gold but have a higher value than pure gold (per ounce) thanks to its desirability as a collector's item. When buying coins, you're also purchasing the desirability of the coin and you should thoroughly evaluate its merits and demerits.

We should also note that contrary to popular belief, you *can* hold physical gold and silver with a self directed IRA or a 401(k) established with a trust company. You cannot buy physical gold with a conventional IRA, because they do not allow for "special circumstances" assets like precious metals. Although you can transfer your current IRA to a self-directed one.

When buying physical gold, it's better to buy workable sizes instead of one huge size. For example, it's better to buy 10 one-oz. bars than to buy one 10 oz. bar. This way you can sell portions of your investment into the market should the need ever arise.

A second way of investing in gold is via ETFs. ETFs vary in terms of the strategies they apply and you should carefully evaluate what these are before investing in them. A lot of ETFs invest in gold futures while some invest in mining companies and so on. Still some more invest in physical gold.

There are a few risks of investing in ETFs. For one thing you won't own the metal directly. In fact, you'll typically be at least two steps removed from it. You'll own shares in a fund that invests in futures contracts. As a result, you might be exposed to the type of price action that oil experienced in the early part of 2020.

Investing in futures also involves what is called counterparty risk. A futures instrument is a contract where one party promises to deliver an asset to the other at a certain price at a certain date. If the counterparty doesn't live up to their end of the deal, there isn't much the other side can do.

Sure, you could go after them, but if they plead bankruptcy, this isn't going to do you much good. Smaller investors won't face such risks because of their investment sizes being small. This is not the case with ETFs that are investing billions in the market. While default isn't something that occurs a lot, there's no denying that during extraordinary times, as most bear markets are, counterparty risk increases significantly.

Another aspect of counterparty risk is the byzantine process by which ETFs actually buy gold. GLD is one of the most popular ETFs when it comes to gold investment.

Here's how the buy chain works. An investor buys shares in GLD. These are delivered by an Authorized Participant to you. This Authorized Participant then buys equivalent shares in the SPDR Gold Trust. The Trust then buys physical gold and stores it with a custodian, in this case HSBC Bank. HSBC also helps source the gold for the trustee. When it comes down to it, the investor is completely dependent on HSBC. Now because most investors buy gold to insulate themselves from financial meltdowns. If there is a meltdown, you can bet that a global bank like HSBC is going to be involved in it somehow. Therefore, investing in gold via an ETF hasn't provided any insulation at all.

The biggest disadvantage to investing this way is that you don't own any physical gold and instead you're investing in the trustee. If there ever comes a time when you need to cash in your gold, you'll be doing so in dollars, which makes you dependent on the monetary system.

Despite the risks, gold ETFs can be good investments. Our point is to highlight the risks to present a well-rounded picture. If you cannot practically buy physical gold, then investing through an ETF makes sense.

An even more indirect way to invest in gold is to buy shares of mining companies and streamers. Let's look at miners first. As the name suggests, these are companies that mine gold and sell it on the market for a profit. Gold mining has very little output and the global supply of gold is pretty low.

South Africa happens to be the largest exporter of gold and it also perfectly illustrates the advantages and disadvantages of investing in miners. On the positive side, you have the fact that you're investing in a company whose product will always have demand. People have been drawn to gold ever since it was first discovered and this is unlikely to stop, no matter how many times Warren Buffett proclaims that gold is useless.

By investing in a miner you're placing your money as close to physical gold as possible. This puts you in a better position than investing in an ETF. The company's prospects are tied quite closely with the price of spot gold since they're selling the raw material for the finished product (gold ore).

The downsides are quite significant, though. You're still intimately tied to the prospects of the mining business. Mining is a capital-intensive business, and it isn't uncommon for mining companies to have low levels of cash the deeper they get into a project. This causes them to seek loans and that builds debt.

While a leveraged balance sheet can produce huge returns for shareholders when things go well, it does open you up to significant downside risk. For example, let's say you buy 1 share of a $100 stock by placing $1 of your own money and borrow the remaining $99. If the stock price increases by one percent to $101, you've just earned a 100% cash on cash return.

However, if it declines by just one percent (to $99), you've lost all of your investment. There's no margin of safety in this case. While the example highlights huge amounts of leverage, the point still stands. A leveraged balance sheet puts the miner at risk. If the ore in the mine doesn't live up to market standards or if a global meltdown happens and secondary effects impact the economy of the industry, the gold miner will likely go bankrupt.

Then there's country risk as well. South Africa, which is where the most prolific miners are located, happens to be particularly unstable when it comes to mining strikes. Workers' rights is a huge issue and it also happens to be racially charged, like everything else in that country. Buying mining stock exposes you to this risk.

Keeping these risks in mind, most miners seek to avoid leveraging their balance sheets. They still need cash, though. This leads them to approach streaming companies or streamers. We highlighted one particularly good streamer in our other book *20 for 20* called Sandstorm Gold.

Here's how streaming works: The streamer provides the miner a loan that is collateralized by the ore that is recovered. The miner agrees to sell the ore at a discount to the streamer. The streamer in turn can either sell the ore or refine it to create pure gold. Since they've bought it at a discount, the streamer realizes significant profits the minute the mine begins producing.

The biggest advantage of the streaming model is that the payouts are connected to the potential of the mine, not the miner. In other words, the miner might run out of cash to refine the ore and could struggle to sell it in the market. This does not concern the streamer since they're receiving the product no matter what.

The streamer thus acts like a bank and receives physical products instead of interest. This aligns their interests with that of the miner without creating heavy dependence on the mining business. As an investor, this is a huge asset for you. This doesn't mean the streaming business is without risks.

For starters, the company might misread the mine's potential output. Secondly, macroeconomic factors might make financing tough for a streamer. These companies typically borrow money from banks, and if banks tighten lending standards far too much, then streamers might not be able to provide miners with financing.

Despite these risks, streaming remains the best method of investing in gold after buying physical gold. There are quite a few companies in this field, but as we have mentioned, Sandstorm Gold is one of the best candidates for investment in this area.

Storing Gold Safely

One of the biggest headaches with gold investment is the storage needs it imposes on investors. This is often why a lot of people prefer investing in ETFs. Gold storage can be tough, but it's hardly a reason for you to stay away from investing in it. The first option is to buy a fireproof safe.

When buying this safe, it's best to pay with cash and install it in your home yourself. The reasons for this should be obvious. Store your gold within the safe at home and you'll always have access to it.

Yet there are downsides to this method. For starters, it's in your home and this makes home security paramount. The very presence of a safe in your home might attract less desirable consequences and your overall peace of mind might be disrupted. After all, your home is a place to relax and feel safe. Storing gold within it might not suit the mindset of most people.

Safety deposit boxes in banks are a favored option. They are cheap and convenient. Most safety boxes cost around $50 per year to maintain and offer large-enough sizes for you to store all the gold you want. But these have significant drawbacks to them. For one thing, these boxes can technically be seized by the government at the stroke of a pen.

This is what happened in 1933 when an executive order signed by President Roosevelt mandated that all gold held in private safety deposit boxes would be seized and that Americans were forbidden from owning gold. The rationale behind this was that people were hoarding gold during the depression and this was making things worse. For people who did comply with the order, the government paid them $20.67 for every ounce of gold that was turned in. But then, shortly after the deadline, Roosevelt raised the price of gold to $35, essentially stealing nearly half of the wealth of those former gold owners.

As far as legally mandated thuggery goes, this act is right up there and there's no reason why it won't occur again. The United States and most Western economies have a checkered record when it comes to this sort of thing. In the name of clamping down on money laundering Americans are now subject to more financial surveillance and heavy-handedness than ever.

For example, the money in your bank account can always be seized by the government and it's technically not yours. If you fall behind on your tax payments, the IRS can seize the money in your account even if this leaves you with nothing to pay for your living expenses.

Aside from the way governments behave there's the fact that the Federal Deposit Insurance Corporation (FDIC) does not insure safety deposit boxes.

The FDIC typically insures bank balances for up to $100,000, but safety deposit boxes are not provided this insurance. This leaves you vulnerable to any misfortune that might befall the bank.

There are private repositories that store gold for you in the United States and offshore. Repositories in the United States are required to comply with income declaration guidelines. This is another way of saying that the government will have full access to your gold much like they have access to your bank accounts.

People who are especially mistrustful of the government can consider offshore storage options. If you're an American resident, your options in this sphere are severely limited. For example, Switzerland offers a range of brokerage and storage services, but many Swiss institutions will not accept American clients due to the demands that income declaration laws place on them. These institutions have built their business on privacy protection and offering governments access to client assets is unlikely to help them.

The best options for American residents (and citizens) is Singapore. The country is a stable financial jurisdiction and its infrastructure is in fact decades ahead of the West. Singapore does not offer the highest levels of protection in terms of privacy, but it does offer you secure storage and a number of companies that offer brokerage services.

Le Freeport in Singapore is an option that many investors utilize. The company has two branches, one in Luxembourg and another in Singapore. Upon visiting you will be guided through a facility that resembles something out of a high-tech spy movie. Costs reportedly start from a few hundred dollars per month for the smallest storage options.

Another storage option exists in Vienna, where investors can have their gold delivered to companies such as Das Safe. In contrast to Singapore, this option adheres to old-school European banking values. One might wonder how much privacy an EU country can provide, but Austria happens to have one of the world's highest priorities in terms of privacy laws.

The costs of offshore storage are higher than what you would have to pay with a storage repository such as Brinks. However, if privacy is a concern for you and if you're really planning for a doomsday scenario, these options are great. Make sure you don't plan on liquidating your asset before you invest in these facilities since they're not the most accessible, thanks to their locations.

POSTMASTER: PLEASE POST IN A CONSPICUOUS PLACE. — JAMES A. FARLEY, Postmaster General

UNDER EXECUTIVE ORDER OF THE PRESIDENT

issued April 5, 1933

all persons are required to deliver

ON OR BEFORE MAY 1, 1933

all **GOLD COIN, GOLD BULLION, AND GOLD CERTIFICATES** now owned by them to a Federal Reserve Bank, branch or agency, or to any member bank of the Federal Reserve System.

Executive Order

FORBIDDING THE HOARDING OF GOLD COIN, GOLD BULLION AND GOLD CERTIFICATES.

By virtue of the authority vested in me by Section 5 (b) of the Act of October 6, 1917, as amended by Section 2 of the Act of March 9, 1933, entitled "An Act to provide relief in the existing national emergency in banking, and for other purposes," in which amendatory Act Congress declared that a serious emergency exists, I, Franklin D. Roosevelt, President of the United States of America, do declare that said national emergency still continues to exist and pursuant to said section do hereby prohibit the hoarding of gold coin, gold bullion, and gold certificates within the continental United States by individuals, partnerships, associations and corporations and hereby prescribe the following regulations for carrying out the purposes of this order:

Section 1. For the purposes of this regulation, the term "hoarding" means the withdrawal and withholding of gold coin, gold bullion or gold certificates from the recognized and customary channels of trade. The term "person" means any individual, partnership, association or corporation.

Section 2. All persons are hereby required to deliver on or before May 1, 1933, to a Federal Reserve Bank or a branch or agency thereof or to any member bank of the Federal Reserve System all gold coin, gold bullion and gold certificates now owned by them or coming into their ownership on or before April 28, 1933, except the following:

(a) Such amount of gold as may be required for legitimate and customary use in industry, profession or art within a reasonable time, including gold prior to refining and stocks of gold in reasonable amounts for the usual trade requirements of owners mining and refining such gold.

(b) Gold coin and gold certificates in an amount not exceeding in the aggregate $100 belonging to any one person; and gold coins having a recognized special value to collectors of rare and unusual coins.

(c) Gold coin and bullion earmarked or held in trust for a recognized foreign Government or foreign central bank or the Bank for International Settlements.

(d) Gold coin and bullion licensed for other proper transactions (not involving hoarding) including gold coin and bullion imported for reexport or held pending action on applications for export licenses.

Section 3. Until otherwise ordered any person becoming the owner of any gold coin, gold bullion, or gold certificates after April 28, 1933, shall, within three days after receipt thereof, deliver the same in the manner prescribed in Section 2; unless such gold coin, gold bullion or gold certificates are held for any of the purposes specified in paragraphs (a), (b), or (c) of Section 2; or unless such gold coin or gold bullion is held for purposes specified in paragraph (d) of Section 2 and the person holding it is, with respect to such gold coin or bullion, a licensee or applicant for license pending action thereon.

Section 4. Upon receipt of gold coin, gold bullion or gold certificates delivered to it in accordance with Sections 2 or 3, the Federal Reserve Bank or member bank will pay therefor an equivalent amount of any other form of coin or currency coined or issued under the laws of the United States.

Section 5. Member banks shall deliver all gold coin, gold bullion and gold certificates owned or received by them (other than as exempted under the provisions of Section 2) to the Federal Reserve Banks of their respective districts and receive credit or payment therefor.

Section 6. The Secretary of the Treasury, out of the sum made available to the President by Section 501 of the Act of March 9, 1933, will in all proper cases pay the reasonable costs of transportation of gold coin, gold bullion or gold certificates delivered to a member bank or Federal Reserve Bank in accordance with Section 2, 3, or 5 hereof, including the cost of insurance, protection, and such other incidental costs as may be necessary, upon production of satisfactory evidence of such costs. Voucher forms for this purpose may be procured from Federal Reserve Banks.

Section 7. In cases where the delivery of gold coin, gold bullion or gold certificates by the owners thereof within the time set forth above will involve extraordinary hardship or difficulty, the Secretary of the Treasury may, in his discretion, extend the time within which such delivery must be made. Applications for such extensions must be made in writing under oath, addressed to the Secretary of the Treasury and filed with a Federal Reserve Bank. Each application must state the date to which the extension is desired, the amount and location of the gold coin, gold bullion and gold certificates in respect of which such application is made and the facts showing extension to be necessary to avoid extraordinary hardship or difficulty.

Section 8. The Secretary of the Treasury is hereby authorized and empowered to issue such further regulations as he may deem necessary to carry out the purposes of this order and to issue licenses thereunder, through such officers or agencies as he may designate, including licenses permitting the Federal Reserve Banks and member banks of the Federal Reserve System, in return for an equivalent amount of other coin, currency or credit, to deliver, earmark or hold in trust gold coin and bullion to or for persons showing the need for the same for any of the purposes specified in paragraphs (a), (c) and (d) of Section 2 of these regulations.

Section 9. Whoever willfully violates any provision of this Executive Order or of these regulations or of any rule, regulation or license issued thereunder may be fined not more than $10,000, or, if a natural person, may be imprisoned for not more than ten years, or both; and any officer, director, or agent of any corporation who knowingly participates in any such violation may be punished by a like fine, imprisonment, or both.

This order and these regulations may be modified or revoked at any time.

FRANKLIN D ROOSEVELT

THE WHITE HOUSE
April 5, 1933.

For Further Information Consult Your Local Bank

GOLD CERTIFICATES may be identified by the words "GOLD CERTIFICATE" appearing thereon. The serial number and the Treasury seal on the face of a GOLD CERTIFICATE are printed in YELLOW. Be careful not to confuse GOLD CERTIFICATES with other issues which are redeemable in gold but which are **not** GOLD CERTIFICATES. Federal Reserve Notes and United States Notes are "redeemable in gold" but are **not** GOLD CERTIFICATES and are **not** required to be surrendered

Special attention is directed to the exceptions allowed under
Section 2 of the Executive Order

CRIMINAL PENALTIES FOR VIOLATION OF EXECUTIVE ORDER
$10,000 fine or 10 years imprisonment, or both, as provided in Section 9 of the order

Secretary of the Treasury.

A reprint of Executive Order 6102 which gave the US Government the legal right to confiscate gold owned by private citizens. The law was in place for 41 years until it was repealed by President Ford. A similar order was signed regarding silver deposits in 1934.

SILVER

Along with gold, silver is another famous precious metal that catches investors' eyes. Unlike gold, silver actually has many industrial uses and has sizable demand from industry. This means its price fluctuates according to supply and demand principles to a larger extent than gold's does.

For this reason, many famous investors recommend silver as being a better investment than gold. Warren Buffett is famous for his disdain of gold but has invested in silver in the past. Historically, silver has been regarded as the second most valuable metal in the world.

Back in the 1800s, the economies of countries were pegged to the levels of silver and gold they held in reserves. This era is often referred to as the bimetallic age. Countries determined how much money they should print on the basis of some combination of the amount of gold and silver they held. This also meant that silver prices were fixed to gold and both metals fluctuated in a correlated manner.

The ratio of gold's price to silver was 15 (Banton, 2020). While the bimetallic method was good in theory, in practical terms it didn't always work out. During this age, European economies were the most advanced in the world and, given the number of conflicts they had with one another, the bimetallic standard was almost never adhered to.

A good example of this is Austria. These days the country is primarily known for Mozart and Freud, but in the 1800s it occupied a position much like America does in the world today. The country went through a century of prosperity in the 1700s and this meant it was embroiled in conflict with its neighbors throughout the 19th century.

The economic history of Austria during this time is a succession of promising to stop printing money and then printing it anyway, followed by head scratching as to why this was done in the first place. War costs money and the economic depression that sets in after it requires money printing.

Since gold and silver reserves were largely fixed, this meant that the Austrian Florin was out of touch with the bimetallic standard. Eventually in 1870, Austria gave up pretending it was following the standard and other European countries followed suit. The constant wars had taken a toll on Austria and the country never recovered its former status in world politics.

The bimetallic era gave way to the gold standard since gold was viewed as being more precious and this gave countries more leeway in terms of how much money they could print. With silver now freed from gold, the gold to silver ratio began to fluctuate.

Over the years, as the 20th century unfolded, the ratio went higher and higher and even reached as high as 100 in 1991. These days the ratio hovers around 50. Of course, countries gave up the gold standard in the 1970s and this has meant the ratio is even more volatile than ever.

Traders seek to take advantage of the gold to silver ratio by adopting mean reversal strategies. This means when the ratio falls far out of line with historical averages, they bet on it moving back to the mean. This isn't an investment strategy, and we won't be focusing on this as a result.

When buying physical silver, you will find that the premium you will be charged over the spot price will be a lot higher than what you'll find in gold. The reason for this is the demand for silver is higher than what exists for gold. The reason silver prices don't go charging up is because silver supply is also relatively high.

Bullion dealers are aware of the fact that silver's industrial usage means demand is strong. Compare this to the situation in gold, where demand is mostly driven by emotional buying. The buyer can always reason that they'll buy it later since they're going to be storing the gold anyway and not putting it to practical use.

This isn't the case with silver. The metal is used in a variety of industrial processes such as in soldering LED chips, creating alloys, creating RFID chips, semiconductors, photovoltaic cells and so on. The metal also has medicinal qualities and is witnessing a surge in nanomedicine.

All of this contributes to you having to pay a higher premium when you invest in it. Historically, there have been many commodity traders who have viewed silver as a better inflation-hedged asset than gold. Their thinking is that since the metal has practical use, it is a better hedge against money printing activities.

This line of thought illustrates the danger of putting too much importance on a fully rational process without taking emotions into consideration. The most famous example of this was the Hunt brothers' corner of the silver market in the 1970s (Beattie, 2019). H.L. Hunt made his money in oil, and upon his passing his sons inherited his considerable wealth.

The Hunt brothers were convinced that silver prices were going to increase rapidly thanks to a weakening dollar and renewed energy crisis concerns. With the United States facing a shortage of oil and inflation at an eye watering 14%, there was a lot of sense in the Hunts' theory. However, much of their execution was flawed.

For starters, it was gold that began rising, not silver. This goes back to our point in the previous section where we mentioned that gold rises in fear. Silver is at a disadvantage in such a scenario. It rises on some occasions and stays flat on others. For example, in 2009 silver began rising along with gold as the credit crisis began hitting home. However, it didn't do so after the dotcom crash.

Either way, the Hunts poured their money into silver and were rewarded with rising prices. Taking this to be a sign, they borrowed money and leveraged their trades. By buying up monstrous amounts of silver in the market, they briefly managed to become the richest men in the world.

However, they created a situation where there were very few counterparties left to trade with. Even worse, the government noticed what they were up to and decided that they were attempting to create a monopoly in silver and strong-arming the economy. This led to a crackdown of biblical proportions, and given the small number of counterparties to their trade, the Hunts had no leverage when it came to negotiating price.

They were forced to declare bankruptcy and were dragged in front of Congress as well. It took them 10 years to get rid of their debts and set things right with their creditors. Don't worry, though. The Hunts made good and became billionaires once again thanks to their oil holdings. They reportedly stayed away from silver after this debacle.

This episode illustrates the irrationality that often afflicts the best investment ideas. The Hunts' thesis specified that things were going to fall apart and didn't account for the government stepping in and changing the rules. While it is unlikely that you'll be playing on the same level as they were, it is something to take note of.

Silver has a lot of things going for it, but just like gold, it is subject to irrationality. Bear markets are highly irrational times. While you can take advantage of this, it might also turn around and bite you if you're not careful.

Let's look at a few ways for you to invest in silver.

Silver ETFs

Like with gold, silver has a number of ETFs that track its price. Just like with gold, there are risks associated with these ETFs. The primary investment reasoning for silver is that it functions as a great hedge. However, with an ETF you're not really gaining much of a hedge. All you're doing is speculating on the price.

The risks associated with silver ETFs are the same as with gold ETFs. We highlighted these risks when looking at the case of GLD in the previous section. Given that silver has a large number of industrial uses, the number of strategies that you'll find in the silver ETF space are high as well.

For example, the iShares MSCI Global Silver and Metals Miners fund (SLVP) tracks a composite basket of silver futures and mining stocks. Buying this ETF will bring you exposure to the entire silver market, but it's a pretty indirect way to invest in the metal itself.

A more direct way is offered by the iShares Silver Trust. This fund functions exactly like GLD does and holds multiple custodian relationships for the storage of silver. However, the risks here are high. Typically, such funds have complex relationships with the custodians of physical silver and in some cases, they might even hire sub-custodians.

These sub-custodians might be located in less than savory places, and as a result there is the danger of fraud occurring. Remember that at the end of the day these ETFs are still funds that operate at the manager's discretion. If the manager decides that the silver market is far too volatile and that palladium offers better opportunities, they can legally shift operations there.

This leaves you in a vulnerable position. When investing in an ETF, what you're actually doing is investing in managerial prowess, not the underlying commodity.

Another silver ETF that is popular is the Global X Miners Silver ETF (SIL). This is an index fund masquerading as an ETF. It tracks an index of silver miners. While this reduces the risk inherent in silver investment considerably, you're still not following the price of silver directly or owning any metal. What's more, this particular ETF has far less liquidity than the others.

Liquidity refers to how readily an instrument trades in the market. An instrument that has just 100 active traders will be less liquid that an instrument that has 1,000 active traders. You're more likely to receive a fair price for your asset if it's liquid. The greater number of traders present will ensure that there will be more prices available for you to buy or sell your asset.

The bottom line is that silver ETFs present a large degree of risk and you should carefully consider your other options before choosing to invest in them.

Mining and Streaming

Like with gold, silver offers a number of opportunities to invest in mining and streaming companies. By investing in these companies you're going to gain exposure to the finances of the individual company and not the metal directly. Silver prices might increase, but if the company mismanages its investments, you could be stuck with a dud.

There's also location risk as we highlighted in the previous section when talking about gold miners. Silver mines are located in even riskier locations across the world. While the world's highest producers of silver are located in Mexico, Peru and China—places that aren't all that unstable—the case of Tahoe Resources illustrates just how risky things can get.

Tahoe Resources, which is now a part of Pan American Silver, was a company that owned and operated a mine named Escobal in Guatemala (Chamaria, 2018). Given the political history of that country and shifting lines of power, it was no surprise that Tahoe had managed to gain access to it under questionable circumstances.

These circumstances perhaps allowed it to operate with impunity for a while, but soon it ran into trouble. A local NGO raised questions about the circumstances under which it was granted a license and soon the case landed in the Guatemalan Supreme Court. This took place in early 2017.

There were other issues as well, mostly to do with the red tape that Tahoe had to navigate. While its mining license was reinstated, its export license that was issued by another ministry was not. This left it in the curious position of being able to mine silver but not being able to do anything with it.

The case was brought to the Supreme Court and the process was expected to take 18 months conservatively. This meant that Tahoe would be offline till the end of 2018. This was a best-case scenario estimate. Ultimately, the management had enough of dealing with third world courts and decided to sell itself to its primary competitor, Pan American, which had a stronger balance sheet and could withstand these shenanigans.

Tahoe's case underlines the importance of doing your due diligence. Companies might have a list of diversified mine locations, but all it takes is for one crackpot government to throw things completely out of shape. In such investments you're dealing with a company that is effectively a foreign stock. After all, the bulk of their assets are outside the USA and in such cases, they're subject to foreign laws.

The company's 10-K will list the production capacity of every mine it has control over. Pay close attention to where it derives the bulk of its production. Mining is a tough business that is constantly plagued by allegations of exploitation and environmental concerns. This is doubly true when operating outside of Western economies.

You want to reduce your risk of exposure towards one particular political climate or zone of the world and invest in companies that have diversified assets. A good candidate for investment is First Majestic Silver (TSE:FR). Despite the word silver in the name, the company derives close to 40% of its revenues from gold mining operations.

Since 2011, the company has been steadily moving away from gold dependence and has been expanding into silver. It was founded back in 2001 by the current CEO, Keith Neumeyer. He's been in charge for this whole period and it's safe to say that he knows how his company runs, backwards.

Stable management is a good sign of a well-run company and First Majestic checks this box. It has a strong balance sheet, which is a great thing for a mining company to possess. The CEO owns close to two percent of the company, which is also a great indication of strength in the company.

Speaking of ownership, the investment case for First Majestic is boosted by the fact that Renaissance Technologies owns this company. Renaissance is a hedge fund that is run by a bunch of math geniuses, and over the years their investment record is unparalleled. A vote of confidence from institutional investors of such pedigree is always a good sign.

2019 was a record-breaking year for First Majestic. A key metric that all mining companies track is the recovery rate. This measures the efficiency of their mining operations. It's a measure of how much metal they could recover from the raw ore. In 2019, First Majestic's recovery rate was an astonishing 86%.

The income statement of the company doesn't provide pretty reading. Critics will point to operating losses in both 2018 and 2019 as well as EBITDA losses of 150 million in 2019. However, dig a little deeper and you'll find that these losses were caused mainly by non-cash expenses such as mine depletion allowances (depreciation for mines).

After accounting for these items, the free cash flow from operations stands at $140 million for 2019, which was up from $33 million in 2018. All of these numbers point to the possibility of a great investment. Given that the pandemic caused by COVID-19 will possibly result in the price of silver rising, this might be a good investment.

Streaming companies are also a good bet in this area. One particularly good company is Wheaton Precious Metals Corp (NYSE:WPM). The economics of silver streamers are the same as those that govern gold streamers. In fact, much like mining companies, streamers tend to invest across both asset classes, so you might end up gaining exposure to gold and silver through these investments.

The bottom line is that there are good opportunities in silver. Remember that ETFs don't always offer the best opportunities. You should look at streamers and a few miners that are well capitalized to take advantage of the potential rise in silver prices.

A historical comparison of the returns of Gold (dark line) vs. Silver (light line) over the past 22 years. A spike in the silver market in 2011 was caused by a supply shortage, rather than the inflationary concerns we saw in the 1980s.

The gold:silver ratio, the number of ounces of silver you can purchase with 1oz of gold. This is a historical indicator going back to Ancient Greece when Alexander the Great fixed the ratio at 12:1. In the modern era, the ratio was initially fixed at 15:1 by the US Government. As countries moved away from the Bi-Metallic age in the late 19th Century, the ratio moved in favor of Gold prices. In the past 20 years, the ratio has been as low as 30:1 during the silver boom of 2011. In the past 12 months we have seen a spike of over 100, a ratio not seen since 1991.

SHORT SELLING

"I've seen more stocks go to zero than infinity."

JIM CHANOS

Let's say you take a look at a company during your analysis and notice that instead of being a gem, it resembles a turd. There's nothing it has going for it and management is incompetent. It's in a business that is stuck in all kinds of difficulties and its competition is pulling ahead.

You'll often come across such companies, and the average investor will simply sigh and move on. After all, there's no point buying these companies. Just because these companies aren't a good buy doesn't mean you can't profit from their situations. This is what short selling is.

The traditional way to make money in the market is to go long. You buy a stock and wait for its price to rise and sell it for a profit. You buy first and sell later. Short selling flips that sequence around. In this method of placing orders, you sell first and then buy. You'll make money if the selling price is higher than what you can buy the stock back for.

Shorting seems like a complicated process, and behind the scenes it is. However, this complexity doesn't need to affect you as an investor. As far as you're concerned, you can sell first and buy later (called covering your short.) You'll need to pay attention to a few things with regards to your account balance, but with prudent risk management, it is possible to do this quite easily.

The biggest qualm most people have with shorting is that they think it's immoral. They think that by shorting you're rooting for someone to fail. This is an uneducated opinion and adopts a very black and white view of the world. A company that is strong and well-run cannot be shorted successfully.

It is impossible for a single trader to ever force prices in the market in a particular direction. As we highlighted earlier, the Hunt brothers managed to buy almost all of the silver in the market and even this didn't allow them to prop prices up. The market is bigger than everyone else.

If the market witnesses unjustified shorting it will react with even greater long pressure. In order to short, you need to have a very strong justification for doing so. It isn't a question of "I don't like the CEO's face hence I'll short." There are urban legends of institutional money managers using shorting as a means of forcing management to bend to their will, but this is mostly false.

Management typically hates short sellers and they're the ones who often peddle the immoral line. Their compensation is tied to stock prices (thanks to options) and any potential reduction in them hurts their wallets. Good management typically doesn't care about shorting activity. It is bad management that always blames shorts for everything.

Some of the most famous investors have made billions shorting. Jim Chanos famously shorted Enron when it was trading at $90 and cleared $500 million from his bet. Going back in time, one of the most famous short sells ever was when Jesse Livermore spotted the signs of the stock market being overvalued in 1929 and shorted the entire market.

Livermore, who is something of a cult figure amongst traders, began by shorting the biggest companies in the Dow Jones index and kept shorting other industries as the malaise spread. By the end of it he had amassed profits of more than $100 million. What is often left out of the story is that he was $6 million in the red before his bet worked in his favor.

In this perfect example of how the mainstream media and uninformed public views shorting, Livermore was blamed for the crash and received death threats. Shorts are simply the messengers of bad news, not the creators of them.

Another example of this comes from 1992 when George Soros shorted the British pound. He cleared $1 billion from this trade and earned the undeserved moniker "the man who broke the Bank of England." This suggests that he somehow bankrupted England by causing a devaluing in the pound, but this simply wasn't the case. If anything, Soros was the one who highlighted the cover-up efforts that the Bank of England was undertaking by trying to smooth over deficiencies in the economy.

There are other notable examples, such as Paul Tudor Jones shorting the American market before the crash of 1987 and Sir John Templeton (him again) shorting the dotcom bubble. While there are many investors who choose to go short, shorting and investing have been viewed as polar opposites thanks to the words of Warren Buffett.

Buffett famously avoids shorting. His reasoning is simple. Stocks can go up infinitely but they're always limited to the downside by zero. Chanos' retort to this is that he's seen many more stocks go to zero than infinity. It just goes to show that sticking to your circle of competence is extremely important in investing.

Many famous investors are conscious of the bad optics that announcing a short brings. As a result, they almost never announce their short positions. In fact, an announcement of this kind by a famous investor can be considered as evidence of financial foul play by the SEC. For example, if Warren Buffett announced he was selling shares of Goldman Sachs, the stock price would tumble.

However, this didn't faze Bill Ackman when he announced his short of Herbalife, Inc. According to him, the company was running a pyramid scheme. He proclaimed that he was going to donate his profits to charity once he was proved true. Ackman appeared on CNBC shortly after this proclamation and reasserted his conviction behind his bet.

This prompted Carl Icahn to phone into the show, and a highly entertaining mudslinging match began between the two rivals. Icahn declared he was going to buy shares in Herbalife just to prove how wrong Ackman was and the stock price of Herbalife began soaring. Other hedge fund managers quietly allied against Ackman as well, with Dan Loeb of Third Point

Partners, who was thought to be Ackman's ally, joining Icahn.

Amidst all this drama was the fact the market deduced that Herbalife was not running a pyramid scheme and Ackman wound up being wrong. He never fully disclosed how much he lost, but one assumes he could afford it (Monica, 2018).

The Basics of Short Selling

As we mentioned earlier, short selling is a straightforward process as far as the investor is concerned. From a bird's eye view, it does get complicated. Here's how it works: You initiate a short by clicking the sell button in the software provided by your broker. If you don't own the stock, your broker has to borrow the shares from someone else to allow you to sell them.

The act of borrowing brings interest with it and your broker will pass this cost onto you. Different countries treat the payment of this interest in different ways. In the United States, the interest is added to the price you pay to enter your trade. If you hold onto your trade for multiple days, your broker will debit the interest from your account.

To close or cover your position, you press the buy button and your broker will take the borrowed shares back and will return it to the source they borrowed it from. This is usually from another trader's margin account or from their own inventory of shares.

If this process sounds confusing to you, think of it this way. Replace shares with money. Let's say you want to borrow $100 (the money that represents a sale of stock). Your broker borrows this amount from another trader or from their own wallet and lends it to you (they've synthetically bought the stock for you).

After a while, you return the $100 back to them (by covering your position you pay them money that represents how much it costs to buy) and the broker returns the borrowed amount to the original source plus interest ("Who Benefits From Loaning Shares in a Short Sale?," 2020).

This is how short selling works on a retail level. At the institutional level, it involves sales and agreements between two counterparties, with the broker acting as an intermediary. In some cases, the broker might take the other side of the trade, but this is done only if the broker evaluates the risk as being worthy of accepting.

Institutional brokers are the big Wall Street banks and typically they don't assume counterparty risk. The exception is when the asset is already on their books and they're looking to get rid of it.

As a retail trader, short selling is extremely easy for you to carry out. The first step you'll need to take is open a margin account with your broker. Margin accounts usually attract higher minimum account balance requirements. Brokers in the United States usually place a threshold of $10,000 for these accounts, but this varies from broker to broker.

Discount brokers sometimes provide margin accounts for as little as $5,000. Opening a margin account is as easy as applying for one through your broker. There is no additional documentation needed beyond what you already provided them when you opened your trading account. Once you have a margin account, you'll be able to not just short sell but also trade futures and options.

Before you proceed to begin trading your margin account it's important for you to understand that Pattern Day Trader rule or PDT. PDT is an SEC-mandated designation that came about because too many retail traders were running huge risks using margin accounts.

If you place more than four trades over the span of five days in your margin account, you'll be slapped with a PDT tag. There is nothing additional you need to do in this case except maintain a minimum balance of $25,000. If you do not comply with these requirements within the mandated time (as defined by your broker), your broker will liquidate your positions and might even freeze your account.

Therefore, if you're going to short sell, be very careful about the PDT rule. If you have that much capital, then you don't have anything to worry about.

The amount of money placed in your account is referred to as the margin you have available. Margin is the sum of your cash balance and the market value of all open positions in your account. If you have a cash balance of $500 and two current positions worth $4,000, your margin is $4,500.

The cash balance is referred to as free margin by some brokers since it represents how much liquid cash you have. Your margin levels are extremely important when it comes to short selling. Let's say you spot a short opportunity that you'd like to use the $500 on.

SEC Regulation T or Reg T specifies that the investor must maintain 150% of the value of short sale in their account as initial margin. In our example, $500 is the value of the short sale and 150% of this is $750. Your account currently has $500 as cash and $4,000 as equity margin. Therefore, you can initiate a short sale.

Once your position is live, maintenance margin requirements go into effect. Maintenance margin refers to the amount of margin your account is supposed to have at all times when the position is open. Currently, the authorities mandate that maintenance margin limits be a minimum of 25% (Kagan, 2020).

However, this is just a minimum. Some brokers will impose maintenance levels of 30%. Coming back to our example, let's say the price of the stock rises (which is bad for a short) and the value of your short position increases to $600. Assuming your broker requires 30% as maintenance margin, you will need to have at least $180 in your account as margin.

Note that this is margin, not cash. Since the other two positions in your account add up to $4,000, you're well above the limit. If you didn't have these two positions in your account, you would have had nothing in your account and would have been hit with a margin call.

This is a notice from your broker asking you to deposit more margin in your account. If you don't do this, your broker will liquidate the position and recover their money from the proceeds. If there were other positions in your account that could allow the broker to recover the maintenance margin amount, your broker will sell those as well.

You need to be very careful of violating maintenance margin requirements. All brokers have an indicator that clearly shows how much equity is left in their account and how close they are to a margin call. Some brokers use a ratio to display this amount. However your broker chooses to depict this, make sure you understand what the indicator means. If you happen to receive a margin call and don't deposit money quickly enough, your broker will sell your investment holdings (even the long ones) and you'll end up losing money.

The Poor Man's Short: Utilizing Inverse ETFs

As you can see, shorting involves a few risks that some investors might not be comfortable with. On top of this, you are not allowed to hold short positions within an IRA because of "undefined risk" rules.

So to aid investors who want to hedge their long-term holds but can't or won't short stocks on margin, many investment managers began offering what are called inverse ETFs. These ETFs, which you are allowed to hold in an IRA, move in the opposite direction to their underlying asset.

For example, ProShare Short QQQ (that's the name; the ticker is PSQ) is an inverse ETF that rises as the NASDAQ 100 falls. If the NASDAQ 100 rises, it falls in price. Another example of this is the ProShares Short Financial Index (SEF). This ETF moves in the opposite direction to the Dow Jones Financial Index.

So if you think financial companies are going to get hammered, you can buy this ETF and put your strategy into action. This is a great way of shorting stocks without requiring a margin account or worrying about maintenance and initial margin requirements.

The correlation between the ProShare Short QQQ inverse ETF and the NASDAQ index between Mar 2008 and Mar 2009. During this volatile period, the inverse ETF returned 14.56% while the index lost 32.74%.

We should note that unless you believe an entire sector is dying, these inverse ETFs are not designed as a long term hold, merely as a hedge against temporary dips in the market. For example, over the past 5 years, the NASDAQ is up 165.82% whereas the inverse ETF is down 65.41%.

Which means you should be wary of such ETFs. When choosing inverse ETFs, stick to the ones that are heavily traded and are the inverse of popular indices. If you find an inverse ETF of a single stock, then run far away from it.

This is because there are many inverse ETFs that are issued by hedge funds. In effect, they're taking the other side of the trade from you. This means you won't have any liquidity when you want to sell and if the position moves against you, you're going to get squeezed.

You'll also find what are called 2x ETFs. These instruments move in double units of their underlying. For example, if the underlying index or stock moves by one dollar, the 2x ETF moves by two. They achieve this through leverage. You'll also find 2x inverse ETFs. If the underlying moves up by one point, the 2x inverse ETF will move down by two.

Stay away from these because leverage ensures you'll get cleaned out quickly. Worst of all, you're not in charge of the leverage and you never know when things might go bad for the fund. In some cases, the government steps in and halts trading in certain instruments if things get out of hand.

For example, in 2008, the government halted trading in SEF, the financial inverse ETF highlighted previously, since all bank stocks were tumbling after the collapse of Lehman Brothers and the credit troubles of the insurance giant AIG.

This means that sticking to broad index inverse ETFs is a good idea. Be on the lookout if things get too grim with a particular sector. It's best to cash out early than risk governmental action that will throw your best-laid plans into a ditch.

The 1 Chart Pattern You Should Know for Short Selling

This isn't a book about technical analysis, but even if you've never utilized charts in your investing philosophy, there is one technical indicator that you should be aware of, and that's the death cross.

The death cross refers to when an asset's short-term moving average crosses its long term moving average. The most common time period for this is when the 50 day moving average falls below the 200 day moving average. In a bull market, both moving averages will rise as there are more buyers than sellers. When the cross happens, it indicates that sellers have recently gained the upper hand and that short-term downwards movements are likely.

The death cross has been a consistent predictor of a number of bear markets including the 1929 crash, the dotcom crash in 2000 and the 2008-9 financial crisis.

For example a death cross occurred on the SPY ETF in mid 2008, at that point the market already had dipped slightly from previous highs, but the index then fell almost 50% from 144.35 to 72.48, and it took almost 18 months for the 50 day moving average to move above the 200 day moving average. This reversal is known as the golden cross.

Another death cross occurred in early 2016, which preceded the small pullback in stock prices over the next 3-4 months. As you can see from the above chart, the death cross is not a 100% accurate predictor of bear markets, and should not be relied upon by itself. If the 50 day average only stays below the 200 day average for a couple of days, then a prolonged bear market is unlikely.

But when it stays there for multiple months, as we saw in 2008, the likelihood of a bear market significantly increases. For example, if you had waited 3 months after the death cross occurred in 2008, you would still have been able to exit SPY at 135, rather than seeing it plummet to 72 within the next 6 months.

We should reiterate that the death cross is not a short term instrument, so you won't be able to day trade on this pattern alone. Nor will you be able to predict events such as COVID-19. Instead it's a tool for long-term investors to take profits before a prolonged bear market is about to begin. Remember, no one ever went broke by taking profits.

INDUSTRIES THAT TRADITIONALLY DO WELL IN RECESSIONS

While shorting is a way for you to take advantage of market weakness, not every company in the market is going to suffer from weak earnings. There are some businesses that do very well in downturns. This section is going to introduce you to a few of them.

Please note that while we'll mention the names of a few companies in this section our objective isn't to provide stock recommendations. It's merely to highlight a few characteristics that we'll be discussing. The focus here is the characteristics, not the companies themselves.

Low Capital Requirements

A bear market places immense strain on all companies in an economy. Cash is hard to come by since lenders have a habit of turning off the supply of money right when people need it the most. In such times, companies that have low costs thrive and ride out the storm far better than the ones that have high costs.

There are two kinds of costs that companies encounter. These are fixed and variable. A mining company, for example, has high fixed costs. Real estate development companies have high fixed costs as well. Variable costs are tied to top line revenues.

For example, the more sales a bakery needs to make, the higher its costs are going to be. Variable costs aren't bad by themselves as long as they're being backed up by higher revenues. The problem arises when companies need to spend additional money to achieve growth. In bull markets such businesses do very well. However, during bear markets such businesses stagnate.

Given that access to financing is so important to these companies, they usually carry high levels of debt in their balance sheets. This comes back to bite them when they cannot earn the same level of return on their investment in a bear market. The aforementioned baker can create all the cakes they want, but try as they might, sales are going to be down.

In bear markets you want to focus on businesses that are service-based and don't require additional investment to provide such services. In-person service businesses tend to do well, but it really depends on the kind of service being offered. Debt consolidation services boom but shoe shining services probably won't.

The COVID-19 pandemic has thrown in-person services into disarray thanks to social distancing requirements. However, as businesses reopen, expect to see a rebound in these sectors. Services these days are provided online as well and these companies have perhaps the best bear market business model.

SaaS or Software as a Service is something we've highlighted previously in this book. By capturing steady monthly payments or by locking in subscriptions for a year, SaaS companies have a strong economic moat. They can scale their business up without having to invest too much into expanding their platform.

For example, the business marketing platform Hubspot is going to encounter similar costs whether 10,000 or 100,000 people use their platform. As user numbers increase they will need more rack space (the technical term for server and data storage space), but these costs reduce on a unit basis over time as more growth is achieved.

These companies also have lower fixed costs. Their business is conducted over the internet which means that the need for physical office space is less. While they will have an office building, the business doesn't depend on having a physical location. Remote work is perfectly fine in such industries and it's no surprise that these businesses have been carrying on as normal (or close to it) during the pandemic.

Traditional businesses will have higher fixed costs than SaaS companies, but this doesn't mean it's a bad thing. It's the ratio of costs to revenues that you want to look at. Retail outlets tend to have high fixed costs, and rent payments make up a large portion of their gross margins.

Even with the move to eCommerce models, the need for inventory storage is high. While the likes of Amazon can thrive thanks to their diversified businesses, the prospects for smaller retail companies aren't as positive.

A significant fixed cost that most investors don't think about often enough is inventory. Inventory on the balance sheet is a double-edged sword. During good times, high inventory levels are a sign of strength, as long as they're in line with revenue growth. When revenue growth stops (during bad times, most likely), the excess inventory becomes a noose.

This is because companies with high fixed costs typically finance inventory creation or purchases with debt. In bear markets, banks will pay closer attention to loan default rates and if a company cannot service their debt, they'll be forced to liquidate inventory and this drastically reduces margins.

Watch out for signs of high inventories on balance sheets, resulting in low net income figures but high cash flow. A drastic decrease in net margin is also a sign of a company liquidating its excess inventory. While inventories might be listed on the asset side of the balance sheet, it can turn against a company quite quickly.

Accounts receivables (the money that is owed to a company by its customers, also called AR) behave in the same manner. During bad times everyone's going to have trouble paying their bills. A large AR figure on the asset portion of the balance sheet might skew the debt to equity ratio favorably.

However, companies that have the majority of their assets tied up in AR or inventory will be forced to bring cash in by renegotiating the terms of payment and might collect 60 cents on the dollar for them. All this does is boost cash flow while doing nothing for profit margins.

Our point is that AR and inventory are costs as well despite being assets. During bad times, even assets can turn against a company and you should consider them to be the equivalent of fixed costs. Stay away from companies that have excessive inventory levels or AR and are unable to move them.

Discounters

One area of business that does very well during bad times are discount retailers. It doesn't matter what is being sold; if they sell items at a discount more often than not, the company will do well. The reasons for this are pretty simple.

With wallets tightening, people will begin to look for lower prices on essential goods. This means they'll turn to discount operators to get the cheapest prices for a variety of items, whether clothes, food, household items, you name it. Retailers such as Walmart, Costco, Dollar Tree and Ross will witness higher foot traffic and revenues in these times.

All of these retailers do have high fixed costs, but the increase in revenues will decrease the cost per unit numbers. Figuring out the cost per unit is a bit difficult for the investor since most companies don't disclose this. This is because it's tough for them to figure out as well.

However, a good substitute is to look at the sales per square foot of retail space and compare that to the fixed cost per square foot. Companies will disclose the total square footage of retail space they have along with the revenues. Costs can be calculated from the income statement by adding the cash cost items. Divide the revenue and costs by the total square footage to arrive at the cost and sales per square foot.

This method isn't foolproof, but in the case of these companies, it will give you an idea of how well the company is maximizing its retail space. Margins in these industries are typically low and the companies here depend on sales volumes. During bear markets, volumes increase rapidly.

The performance of Wal-Mart, Ross & Dollar Tree vs. the S&P 500 from June 2005 to June 2010. Notice the immediate divergence in mid 2008 as the effects of the financial crisis began taking shape, and the shift in spending habits towards discount retailers began. The returns over the 5 year period were as follows

- Dollar Tree: 173.99%
- Ross: 89.89%
- Wal-Mart: 10.3%
- S&P 500: -7.13%

Companies that have a good economic moat will do well in the long run. An economic moat is an advantage that the company has as part of its business model. In Walmart's case, its sheer size gives it a considerable moat. This allows it to negotiate prices with suppliers to rock-bottom levels, and it allows them to purchase large quantities of stock.

This means items never run out and the shopping experience is always consistent. Smaller retailers cannot compete against this. Amazon employs the same model in the eCommerce sector.

Despite the clear advantages of companies like these, some investors might feel that placing their money in one company might be too risky. Bear markets are unpredictable and analyzing a single company requires investing a lot of time that they don't have. If this is the case, investing in Real Estate Investment Trusts (REITs) are a good option. A REIT is a company that owns real estate properties and earns income by maintaining the property.

For example, a REIT could own a large number of apartment complexes. It earns money by collecting rent from these complexes and its costs include office space and maintenance. An investor that buys shares in the REIT is tying themselves indirectly to the performance of those apartment complexes.

This is an indirect method of owning real estate and is a lot cheaper than having to make a down payment for a property. REITs have a number of concentrations. There are diversified REITs that invest in all kinds of properties and specialized REITs that invest in specific types of properties.

There are REITs that invest solely in real estate leased to discount store operators. The Tanger Factory Outlet Stores REIT (NYSE:SKT) is an example of a company that does this. The company owns 39 outlet centers spread across the US, and considers its business model to be one which thrives in market downturns. CEO Steven Tanger famously stated "In good times, people like a bargain. In tough times, people need a bargain"

What makes these companies good investments is that they tend to fall initially in a bear market thanks to the general selling that the overall retail sector faces. During the initial phase of a bear market pretty much every retail stock nosedives since investors believe that people will spend less money shopping. This leads many unintelligent investors to sell discount retailer stocks as well. These companies therefore end up becoming bargains.

This doesn't mean you should buy every single discount retailer REIT out there! It just means that you're more likely to find a bargain in this sector than in other areas. The best part about REITs is that they are legally mandated to pay out 90% of their profits to their shareholders.

Note that it's 90% of profits, not rent. Rent money represents revenues for REITs. They subtract their office and salary costs before passing on 90% of the rest to you. The dividends that you will receive will make for good supplemental income in bear markets and are a great passive income stream.

There is one thing you should be aware of when it comes to looking at REITs. When you look at them in financial screening software, you'll notice that their payout ratios will seem unsustainable. The payout ratio is calculated by dividing the dividend paid per share by the net income earned per share. You want to see stable payout ratios.

In the case of a REIT, you'd expect it to be around 90% since this is what the law says they must do. However, you'll often see numbers that are above this, even reaching 150%. How can a REIT pay more than what they earn?

The answer lies in the way GAAP treats assets. GAAP mandates that all assets on a balance sheet be depreciated over time. This includes property as well. However, as everyone knows, property appreciates over time, especially if it's well maintained. The depreciation expense that REITs take on their income statement is not real. Sure, there's wear and tear over time, but it hardly occurs on the scale that depreciation expense indicates.

This means the cash flow that a REIT collects is the true net income figure, specifically the free cash flow earned after subtracting capital expenditures from cash flow derived from operations. Both of these are line items in the cash flow statement. Look at the dividend payment with respect to this number instead of comparing it to net income.

Pro tip: If you buy REITs within a Roth IRA, you won't pay any capital gains tax or taxes on dividends. Over time, this is hugely beneficial to your overall profits.

Relaxation and Escapes

When speaking of relaxation and escapes you might think cruises and vacation company operators, but remember we're in a bear market. People don't have the same level of disposable income, and these particular industries will be hard hit as you'll shortly learn.

Given that people need to make do with less, you need to focus on companies that make products that allow people a cheap escape. This means brewery companies such as Anheuser-Busch (EBR:ABI) and Constellation Brands (NYSE:STZ) will see increased consumption of their brands.

You might think that people will reduce consumption of such products in tough times given their relative cost, but remember that this is all about providing an escape. For this same reason, tobacco companies witness a surge in demand in tough times despite the increasingly high costs of their products.

A new entrant into this space is the cannabis industry. While the average cannabis company stock experienced a huge surge upwards thanks to impressive marketing and the novelty factor, you can expect the better-run companies to experience increased demand from the public.

Speaking of escapes, companies such as Netflix (NASDAQ:NFLX) and other streaming device manufacturers such as Roku (NASDAQ:ROKU) will also witness an increase in demand. With less money available for going out to movies or spending a night out, you would expect people to stay at home and stream entertainment.

Keep in mind that there are other business factors to take into consideration. Netflix might witness a surge in demand, but does this mean it will do better than its competitors? It may or may not. It depends on how well the company is run and whether it is able to recover costs. Increased demand isn't the only deciding factor when you are looking to invest in a company. It's merely the starting point for you to begin your research.

A significant competitor to Netflix is Disney (NYSE:DIS), and this company always gets hit hard during bear markets. This is because everyone associates it with Disneyland. While the theme parks do account for a significant portion of revenues, this is hardly the only source of income.

Disney is an entertainment giant. It dominates the world of movies (Marvel, Pixar) television (ABC, Disney channels) and sports (ESPN) over and above children's entertainment. The only industry it hadn't expanded to was streaming, and with the launch of Disney Plus, it's expanded there as well.

In bear markets, the stock gets hammered due to decreased Disneyland visits. However, its vast content library and intellectual trademarks ensure that the cash always flows in steadily. It might be a good prospect to look into in bear markets.

In this category we also have adult entertainment companies such as RCI Hospitality Holdings (NASDAQ:RICK). The name of the company is appropriately boring but it includes brands such as the famous Rick's bar in New York City. There are other companies in this space that deserve a second look as well.

Some investors will have ethical concerns over investing in the majority of the industries profiled here. Remember that it isn't 100% necessary to invest in these industries in order to make money. There are many other options as you've already learned. The key is to stick to what you can analyze.

If you're uncomfortable with a business or find it too complex to fully get a handle on, feel free to skip it. There are abundant opportunities in bear markets for you to take advantage of. Our aim is to merely highlight all of these opportunities that are available.

INDUSTRIES THAT ARE HIT THE HARDEST

From industries that perform the best in a downturn we now turn our attention to the ones that are hit the hardest in a downturn. Stay away from investing in these industries and you'll do yourself a massive favor. A lot of these industries come up with spectacular investment offers during such times.

However, these offers do not provide the investor adequate protection from the poor economics inherent in these businesses.

Airlines

Airlines are curious businesses. They're proof of the fact that high demand alone does not sustain a business. We've highlighted previously the case of Concorde. Passengers were extremely happy with their experience on the plane and the aircraft drastically reduced flight time between two of the major financial centers of the world. Yet it still failed.

The demand for air travel has always been high. In the early days of commercial aviation, this was seen as a buccaneering space with the likes of Howard Hughes' Trans World Airlines and Juan Trippe's Pan American Airways battling for supremacy. In the background were dozens of regional airline companies that also competed for space.

All of these companies are distant memories now, and the American aviation industry is a case of choosing the least bad experience possible. It's as if misery is a given on these flights and the worldwide reputation of America's airline companies is terrible. Having said that, examining the state of the industry worldwide doesn't provide a much better picture.

The space is dominated by airlines that are backed by wealthy governments or those that are subsidized by them. Looking at the list of the best airline companies in the world is instructive. Here are the top five from 2019 (Logan, 2020):

1. Qatar Airways - Backed by the government of Qatar, a natural gas-rich monarchy
2. Singapore Airlines - Backed by the government of Singapore, another rich country
3. ANA - A private airline
4. Cathay Pacific Airways - Privately owned, but the Chinese government owns a significant stake through Air China
5. Emirates - The original government-owned airline, backed by the government of Dubai

In addition to these, recall some of the best-known airline companies in the world. Southwest, Ryanair, Air Asia, British Airways and Air France come to mind. All of these, including the ones in the list above are either budget airlines or are government-owned.

The message is clear here. If you own an airline and aren't a budget operator or backed by the government, you're dead in the water. The economics of the commercial aviation industry are so bad that even during the best of times, airline executives whine about the high cost of business.

They're obsessed over their competition at all times and this by itself is a good indication of how well the business runs. A good business doesn't need to worry about its competition. When was the last time you heard Amazon whining about Facebook, Apple or Google?

However, the likes of Delta (NYSE:DAL), American (NYSE:AAL), and United (NASDAQ: UAL) have repeatedly launched attacks on the "Middle Eastern" (their words, not ours) carriers in an attempt to drum up nationalist sentiment against them (Dastin & Saleem, 2015). They somehow overlook the fact that people don't like to be bodily thrown out of their aircraft and put their failure down to sinister government forces, oil price manipulation and so on.

Some investors view airlines as being cyclical stocks. They fall to low levels during downturns and then rise as the economy gets better. In our view, this is little better than trying to time the market. If you're going to invest like this, you might as well try to trade the daily charts.

Even the best investors are susceptible to the glamor that owning an airline brings. One of Warren Buffett's famous mistakes involved U.S Airways in the early 1990's. Charlie Munger quietly quipped that Buffett hadn't consulted him on that one. More recently, Buffett once again invested in all the major airlines only to have his thesis shattered by the COVID-19 crisis.

The fact that he bought them for low prices even before the crisis hit, is a marker of how terrible airline companies are. We mentioned the economic moat previously. It turns out that airlines have a nonexistent moat. Ask yourself: Unless incentivized by miles, would you ever choose to pick United over any of the other airlines available? What's more, miles redemptions have decreased in value thanks to increased competition and price comparison websites.

Your primary decision is based on the price you receive. Whoever offers the lowest price wins your business. As Buffett once famously said when discussing the operations of Berkshire's textile mills (Green, 2016), "When a management with a reputation for brilliance tackles a business with a reputation for poor fundamental economics, it is the reputation of the business that remains intact."

Hotels

Coming close in second place to airlines in the worst business sweepstakes are hotels. While the margins of most hotels aren't as bad as the ones airlines face, the hotel industry is a tough business. It is a business that relies on discount pricing but has to maintain the facade of luxury nonetheless.

Much like airlines, the hotel businesses that do well tend to have a lot of history or backing behind them. The hotel industry is dominated by a small number of conglomerates, such as Hilton (NYSE:HLT) and Marriott (NASDAQ:MAR). There are a few regional brands that displace them, but these are the major players.

All of them have similar business models in that they lease their name to facilities around the world and collect royalties on the brand name. This means these brands have reduced their operational expenses significantly and have removed the risk of having a failed property on their portfolio.

Understanding this decision is a good way of figuring out the economics of the business. If someone approached you with an offer to start a great business with your name on it in another part of the world, you'd most likely jump at the offer. This is assuming the business is in your circle of competence and you've conducted your research into the area.

For example, McDonald's owns all of its restaurant locations. By owning the property, it commits itself to creating a great business wherever it goes. Hotel operators don't do this. Why would they choose to avoid it? Why would you choose to avoid such opportunities from the example in the previous paragraph?

It's probably because the cost of failure and the probability of failure is too high. You'd avoid a deal that is a terrible one. However, hotels have to keep running their business, and as a result they franchise themselves. From the franchisee's perspective, assuming the costs of running a restaurant is a lot lower than assuming the costs of running a 100-room hotel.

The poor economics of running a hotel can be better understood by looking at the work involved in running an Airbnb business. We're not referring to letting out your own property on the platform. Instead, we're talking about offering a handful of owner-owned properties and collecting profits on the price difference in rent you get paid versus the rent you pay.

It is a full-time business to say the least. Your fixed costs are going to be extremely high and you'll have to carry out constant maintenance of the property. You'll need to deal with empty premises and have to market the property to ensure a good flow of tenants. You'll have to pay the rent to the landlord no matter what or else you'll lose the property and your source of income.

Now imagine having these problems multiplied by 100 and having to bear staff salaries and increased marketing costs thanks to competition. You'll also have to deal with regulation since you can't offer just any room as a hotel room for rent. It's little wonder that hotel operators have constantly lobbied governments against platforms such as Airbnb.

As we mentioned in the previous section, a reliable indicator of a business with terrible economics is one where the major executives are either asking for handouts all the time or are engaged in lobbying to pass laws that cripple their competition. The hotel industry doesn't have as poor a reputation as airlines do, but their actions speak loudly.

One particular offer that all hotel operators come up with during tough times is to offer "investment" opportunities in their properties. The marketing material typically highlights the amazing chance to own a room in a five-star property, fully serviced. What's more, the owner can earn rent thanks to the room being rented out. Maintenance is fully taken care of, and the owner can occupy it whenever they wish.

What's worse is you'll be tying yourself to one particular location and will be at the mercy of the hotel's business. Don't even think about such offers.

Both airlines and hotels are ideal condition industries, in short. They need a lot of things to line up in their favor in order to make money. If even one of these things goes slightly off-balance, they lose money. Given the volatility that bear markets introduce to the system, you can bet that these businesses will be the first ones to feel the pinch.

Casual Dining

The casual dining sector is a no man's land. It isn't upscale enough to warrant high prices (think Ruth's Chris) and neither is it cheap enough like fast food to justify repeated visits. A lot of these mid-range dining options incorporate the worst of both worlds.

You pay a higher price to be seated at a table only to be delivered potentially microwaved food. During good times, it's a decent option for a night out and you don't have to spend too much money for family entertainment. During bad times, the negatives of these establishments comes to mind and consumers stay away.

A good example of how badly these companies get hit is Red Robin Gourmet Burgers (NASDAQ:RRGB). The company is in the same space of operations as Chili's, Applebee's and Olive Garden. Once the lockdowns that were prompted by the COVID-19 crisis began, the stock price fell from $30 to $5 over the course of two weeks.

The majority of this price drop was caused by investors overreacting to bad news, to be certain. However, the price as of this writing has barely recovered to $12. These mid-range restaurants have the fixed costs of their higher-priced counterparts in terms of kitchen, real estate and employee salaries. However, their margins are much lower due to the items on their menus being priced lower.

They don't have much brand recognition and struggle to separate themselves from one another. Nor do they have huge fan followings. In order to entice customers to visit them over another brand, they need to offer discounts or special promotions. Olive Garden is particularly famous for this.

Unlimited breadsticks are a promotion that the company uses to lure patrons in. However, these breadsticks don't get them spending more. After all, anyone who eats a large amount of bread before their meal isn't going to spend much on entrees or desserts. Then there's the fact that abusing the breadstick policy at Olive Garden is a cult topic.

Stories abound of people hiding them in their bags and entire threads on Reddit are dedicated to instructing people in the art of maximizing breadsticks. The chain also runs yearly promotions such as bottomless salads and unlimited pasta bowls. These usually attract college students who are unlikely to be repeat patrons.

While Olive Garden's promotions are the most famous example, other chains run similar promotions all the time. Thanks to their menus failing to make any impact with patrons, these companies need to reinvest money to upgrade or change them every few months.

It makes for a tough time if you're an executive of the company. As an investor, you'll constantly be on the lookout for the next downturn so that you can exit as quickly as possible. Some investors might believe these stocks are cyclical, but not every single company adheres to this pattern.

They usually bounce back only when things are going really well and the bull market is already well established. If the bull market happens to be short, then these companies will be stuck in a seemingly perennial rut.

Landlords

What happens the minute people begin to lose jobs? They stop paying rent and other bills. This hits landlords and landlord-related businesses the hardest. The number of vacancies increases and foreclosures increase. Rents might drop, but this depends on how bad the economy gets.

This is a second order effect of a bear market or economic downturn. The real estate cycle doesn't move in the same one as the stock market does. However, it does get affected. Residential real estate is usually hit the hardest and it follows more of a boom and bust cycle than its commercial counterpart.

Residential real estate depends heavily on average consumers having enough money to make mortgage payments and down payments. With money scarce, home purchasing hits record lows. As a result, home builders slow down the pace of development and this hits their business hard.

Recovery is also questionable when it comes to home building companies. They tend to experience the worst of both the stock market and real estate cycles. From the market peak of 2007 till 2020, not a single home building company's stock outperformed the market except for NVR, Inc. (NYSE:NVR)

This has a knock-on effect on companies that are suppliers to home builders. Building materials suppliers such as Caterpillar (NYSE:CAT) and Sherwin Williams (NYSE:SHW) face problems. Other home builders such as Pulte group (NYSE:PHM) and D.R. Horton (NYSE:DHI) also face headwinds.

These days, real estate has moved online and there has been a lot of talk of how the realty industry has been disrupted. This isn't true. The likes of Zillow (NASDAQ:ZG) front themselves as being technology companies but are realtors at heart. The technology angle allows them to push a narrative that gets them valued at higher earnings in the stock market. However, Zillow is still affected by the same cycle as these other companies, regardless of how disruptive it claims to be.

Big box retailers also suffer, especially those catering to home maintenance and contracting. Home Depot (NYSE:HD) and Lowe's (NYSE:LOW) are examples of these.

Despite residential real estate being hit the hardest, commercial real estate gets hit as well. While it does not follow the same boom and bust cycle of residential property, commercial properties tend to get hit hard. REITs that focus on commercial properties especially suffer.

Companies such as Brookfield Group (NYSE:BAM), Simon Property Group (NYSE:SPG) and Macerich (NYSE:MAC) absorb the impact of a slowing retail sector. Less spending means less rental payments made on time. Office space leasing also slows down thanks to the prospect of layoffs and bankruptcies.

A good way to take advantage of these downturns is to purchase an inverse ETF or short the individual stocks. You could also short ETFs that track a commercial real estate index. Whatever method you choose to employ, remember to conduct thorough research into the instrument and understand what you're gaining exposure to.

Delayed Purchase Eligible Products

These products cover a wide range of industries, but their underlying theme is the same. All of them can be bought down the road if money is tight. They aren't products that are necessary and can be considered luxuries. Don't let the word luxury fool you. This doesn't mean companies such as LVMH or Ferrari will struggle.

Truly luxurious items will always have a market since there will always be people with enough money to afford them. Besides, those products do not depend on the bull and bear market cycle anyway. By luxuries, we meant products that are "wants" as opposed to "needs."

A smartphone is a need, but is an iPhone one? If money is tight, even the most rabid Apple fanboys will reconsider their decision to spend money on them. They will either delay the purchase of a new phone for a year or will borrow money through a payment plan to finance the purchase. This may not be the smartest of decisions, but this isn't a book about personal finance.

The companies that make these products will feel the pinch since there's less revenues coming in, even if products are being shipped. The other factor that affects these purchases is that credit card delinquencies typically rise during a bear market.

The pandemic has currently created a bear market and right on cue, credit card delinquencies have risen to their highest point since 2013 ("Delinquency Rate on Credit Card Loans, All Commercial Banks", 2020). Meanwhile, household debt reached record levels in February, when things were still relatively stable (Marte, 2020)

Combine this with an economic recovery over the past decade that was a sham, and you have a perfect situation for spending patterns to change in the coming years. Households will seek to save more money moving forward in anticipation of the next shock.

USING SECTOR SPECIFIC ETFS AS A HEDGE

Capitalizing on bear markets will require you to expand your circle of competence. In some cases, you will find that the instruments in question will be difficult for you to understand fully. In such situations one option for you to utilize would be to invest in ETFs that provide you with exposure to that sector or opportunity.

This will help you stay away from instruments that are too complex or from sectors whose economics you aren't intimately familiar with. The ETFs highlighted in this section will help you hedge against the falling market. You can also use them as long term investments that will remain stable.

Treasury Bills, Notes and Bonds

We've explained what T-bills are previously. These are bonds that are issued by the U.S. Government and form one of the most secure forms of debt in the world. The word "bill" in the name indicates that their maturity is less than a year. These bills have a few quirks to them, and it's worth taking the time to understand how they work.

Bonds are a form of debt. The issuer of the bond borrows money from you when you buy the bond. For example, if company X issues bonds worth $5 million, they're looking to borrow that amount from investors. An investor buys one of these bonds and earns an interest rate that will be paid by the issuer. This interest rate is referred to as the coupon.

The price of a bond fluctuates since it can be traded in the open market. This is true of T-bills as well. This means the bond's yield fluctuates. A bond's yield is a measure of the return the investor will receive if they purchase the bond at the current price. For example a bond that costs $1,000 and pays $10 in annual coupon payments is yielding one percent.

It's important to note that the face value of a bond can be different from its price. The bond from the previous example might be trading currently at $1,000, but it could have a face value of $1,500. When the bond matures, or reaches its expiry date, the issuer returns the face value of the bond to the current owner.

This means investors can earn significant capital gains from speculating on bond prices as well. In practice, this is tough to do and the average investor is best off staying away from such speculation due to the risks involved. T-bills work slightly differently from regular bonds.

For starters, since their maturities are just for one year at most, they don't pay coupons. The government sells them at a discount from their face value and promises to repay the face value upon maturity. The yield is calculated as being the difference between the face value and the discounted value.

The government lists the current T-bill rates at https://www.treasury.gov/resource-center/data-chart-center/interest-rates/Pages/TextView.aspx?data=billrates. Currently, the one-month T-bill is selling at a 0.1% discount to its face value and the one-year bill is selling at a 0.18% discount. As you can see, the returns aren't exactly earth-shattering. However, that's not the point of a T-bill.

As a creditor to the American government, you're backing the most transparent and robust financial system on the planet. Despite rising debt levels, it's unlikely that the American government is going to default on these payments anytime soon.

You can purchase these bills directly from the government at published rates or you can enter a competitive auction. The most common and practical way for a retail investor to purchase T-bills is through an ETF. You buy shares in the ETF and the fund holds previously issued T-bills.

T-notes, or Treasury notes, are bonds that have maturity dates between one and 10 years. These function like normal bonds as detailed previously. The investor receives a coupon payment every year. Typically, the government issues notes with maturity terms of two, three, five, seven and 10 years (Chen, 2020).

T-bonds, or Treasury bonds, have maturities that are above 10 years and run up to 30 years. Currently the 30-year T-bond is yielding 1.44% while the five-year note is yielding 0.34%. All of these instruments are safe havens and are considered to be a safe place to hold cash while the rest of the market declines.

The noteworthy point about all of these instruments is that the gains on them are not taxable. After all, you're funding the government by buying them. Something to keep in mind when buying bonds is the relationship between interest rates and bond prices. They move in opposite directions from one another.

As interest rates rise, bond prices fall. Here's why this happens. Let's say you buy a T-note that is paying you a 0.12% coupon. It's paying you this much because that's the rate fixed by the U.S Federal Reserve Bank (the Fed). During tough economic times, interest rates are slashed to low levels, as you've learned already.

Once times get better, interest rate levels are raised. This means the new T-notes that are issued will pay higher coupons, perhaps 0.2%. Holders of the older notes are therefore losing out. This makes the old notes unattractive and everyone will buy the new notes.

If you hold on till the maturity of the note, you will realize a yield equal to the coupon rate since you'll receive the face value back. Unless you plan on selling the bond before maturity, you don't have anything to worry about.

However, you should be aware of this phenomenon.

Like with T-bills, you can gain exposure to bonds and notes through ETFs. There are three ETFs in particular that have proven themselves to be reputable. Keep in mind that by owning these ETFs you're not owning any bonds or fixed-income instruments. Instead, you're gaining exposure to the yield curves of these instruments.

If the interest rate scenario explained previously happens, the price of the ETF will fluctuate depending on what the manager decides to do. If they dump the old notes in favor of the new, prices will rise. However, if they sell too much, they'll take too large a capital loss and the ETF price will fall.

This makes it imperative for you to choose ETFs that have been run by experienced managers who have a proven track record. The three ETFs below satisfy this criteria:

1. TLT
2. SHY
3. EDV

TLT is the iShares 20+ Year Treasury Bond ETF. The ETF tracks the performance of an index tied to U.S. Treasury Bonds with maturities of greater than 20 years. The fund has returned 9.46% over the past 10 years.

It currently has over $18 billion in assets and is one of the largest ETFs that is currently listed on the NASDAQ. Investors will have to pay 0.15% of their capital invested in the fund as fees every year. This is called the expense ratio. Currently, the fund holds a 99.3% exposure to U.S. Bonds with the remaining 0.7% held as cash.

SHY is the iShares 1-3 Year Treasury Bond ETF. As the name suggests, the fund invests its money in T-notes with a maturity of one to three years. It has returned 1.31% over the past 10 years. The underlying index it tracks is the ICE U.S. Treasury 1-3 Year Bond Index and it has lagged behind this benchmark slightly over the past decade.

It currently has over $23 billion under management. Like the previous ETF, SHY also has an expense ratio of 0.15%. It currently holds a 98.48% exposure to T-notes with the rest held in cash.

EDV is the Vanguard Extended Duration Treasury ETF. Given that this fund is a Vanguard product, it functions as a pure index fund. The underlying index it tracks is the Bloomberg Barclays U.S. Treasury STRIPS 20-30 Equal Par Bond Index. That's quite a mouthful, but the index simply tracks the yields of 20-30 year T-Bonds.

It currently holds over $3.2 billion in assets and has returned 12.57% over the past decade. It has the lowest expense ratio of the trio with just 0.07%. It currently holds 100% of its funds in U.S. Bonds.

None of the above returns are particularly groundbreaking, but that's not the point. The point is that these funds should give a better return than merely holding cash during an economic downturn. Once market conditions begin to improve, then you can sell your holdings in these funds and move more of them into traditional stocks and ETFs.

Consumer Staples

Consumer staples are products that are essential household goods. Groceries, hygiene products and beverages come under this category. As their name suggests, they'll always be in demand no matter what is going on with the economy. The rationale behind buying shares of discount retailers is that cheap consumer staples will always face increased demand during tough times.

Despite the demand for consumer staples remaining constant, there is the danger of prices not matching consumer expectations. If store A stocks a product at $5 and store B stocks it for $6, A will receive the bulk of the business. This makes consumer staples an extremely price-sensitive segment.

The danger for the investor is that they might end up investing in a store or retailer that doesn't offer the lowest prices. This opens them up to huge levels of risk should the underlying economics of that business change. It's far less risky to instead gain exposure to consumer staples as a whole instead of concentrating holdings in one particular company.

This is where the XLP ETF comes into the picture. The underlying index it follows is the Consumer Staples Select Sector Index. This index is a collection of all the consumer staples companies listed in the S&P 500. The companies retail products that range from grocery stores to beverages, other food products, tobacco, personal hygiene products and household products.

It currently has over $14 billion in assets under management. This money is spread over 33 stocks. The highest weighted stock in its portfolio is Procter & Gamble, which is 15% of the overall portfolio, with PepsiCo, Coca-Cola and Wal-Mart also making up a large proportion of its holdings. It has an expense ratio of 0.13% and has returned 10.72% over the past decade.

Healthcare

Healthcare is something that people will always need. From pharmaceutical companies to hospitals to pharmacies, healthcare is a massive sector. Recently, healthcare has been evolving from a person-to-person model to an online model. Teleconsultations have been on the rise over the past decade and the sector is rapidly changing.

Given the large number of companies that operate in the sector, it can be tricky to get your portfolio allocation right. This is where the XLV ETF comes into the picture. Much like the ETF highlighted when we looked at consumer staples, XLV offers the investor exposure to 61 companies in the healthcare field.

The fund has over $26 billion in assets under management and has returned a healthy 14.4% over the past decade. It has an expense ratio of 0.13% and pays a quarterly dividend. Its underlying index is the Health Care Select Sector Index which comprises the biggest stocks in the healthcare sector.

The dividend yield is currently 1.39%, which puts it on par with most common stocks. It has exposure to companies such as Johnson & Johnson, Pfizer, Merck etc.

Safe Dividend Yield

Earning a stream of passive cash flow is pretty attractive for most investors. Dividend paying stocks are sought after for a variety of reasons. Historically, they've outperformed the rest of the market during bear market declines. Their ability to produce income sometimes indicates a core business that is stable.

For example, companies such as Coca-Cola pay steady dividends thanks to their large balance sheets and well-established earning advantages. The downside of investing in a single common stock is that you're gaining exposure to the economics of that particular company. We saw the results of this in Q2 of 2020 as many companies, including Royal Dutch Shell, Dunkin' Brands and General Motors, cut or suspended their dividend due to the COVID-19 pandemic.

In bear markets, ETFs come to the rescue once again if you wish to capture the advantage of steady dividend payouts without having to run the risk of downside exposure in common stocks.

SDY is a famous ETF that offers investors exactly this advantage. The ETF tracks the S&P Dividend Aristocrats Index. This index is composed of companies that have large market size and have paid increasing dividends for at least 25 years. Some companies in this index, such as Coca-Cola and Kimberly Clark, have paid dividends stretching back over 50 years.

It currently has over $15 billion in assets under management and has an expense ratio of 0.35%. It is currently yielding a healthy 3.09%. It has returned 9.87% over the past decade and has distributed its assets across 119 companies. SDY usually sells for prices that place its yields around one to two percent. The current bear market has provided investors a great opportunity to enter.

The US Dollar

We've discussed assets ranging from equities to fixed income thus far. Currencies are another asset class, but they tend to be highly speculative. This is why the average investor is best served by staying away from them. Currencies don't have any value by themselves.

They derive their value in relation to other currencies. When traders speculate in the forex markets, it is the exchange rate they're betting on. Typically, currency investments require huge degrees of leverage because the underlying exchange rates move so little.

Betting directly on currencies, not the exchange rates, is an expensive prospect for the average investor. The amount of capital needed to do this is exorbitant. However, if you have a view on the U.S. dollar, there is a way for you to bet on its strength.

UUP is an ETF that allows you to do just this. The underlying index this fund tracks is a bit complex, but the gist of it is that it tracks the strength in the U.S. dollar (and weaknesses). If the dollar grows stronger, UUP rises in value and if it grows weak, UUP falls.

It currently has $868 million under management and has a high expense ratio of 0.79%. Over the past decade it has returned 1.45%. Keep in mind that the prior decade witnessed a strong bull market and the dollar held its value throughout this. A bear market might result in other currencies weakening, and given the dollar's position as the world's preferred trade currency, one might witness an upswing in prices.

This fund is not a long-term hold since over the long term equities outperform currencies by some distance. However, for periods of three years and under, UUP is a good bet should you want to add US dollar exposure to your portfolio.

Volatility

Another way to protect your portfolio during uncertain times is by profiting from an increase in market volatility. The Chicago Board Options Exchange (CBOE) created an index which tracked the volatility of the overall market, known as VIX. This index tracks the market's expectation for volatility in the next 30 days.

We've previously discussed how bear markets often move more sharply than bull markets. During these times, VIX tends to spike. Which means VIX is inversely correlated with equity prices.

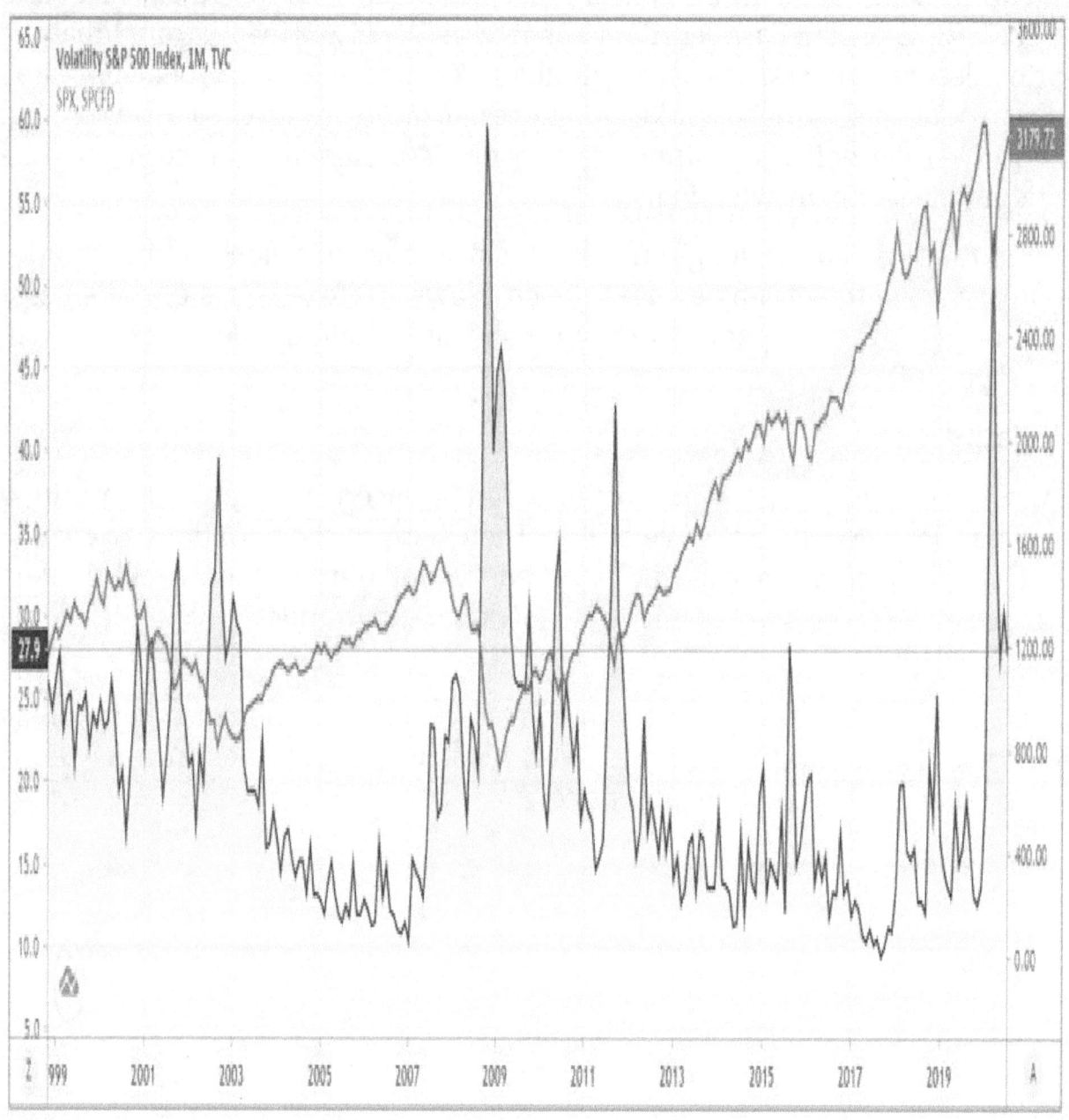

From this chart you can see how VIX spikes as equity prices decrease. March 2020 saw VIX hit an intraday level of 82.69, a level not seen since 2008. As prices climbed from 2012 to the beginning of 2020, VIX remained relatively low, with short spikes during market corrections.

You cannot directly access the VIX index, however one way to profit from this volatility is to use an Exchange Traded Note (ETN) which trades in a similar pattern to VIX. ETNs operate in a similar manner to ETFs, however the main difference is that they do not own the underlying asset.

One such ETN is iPath S&P 500 VIX Short-Term Futures ETN, which trades under the symbol VXX. This product consists of 1 month and 2 month VIX futures contracts, and trades in line with the VIX itself. Which means that in bear markets, as VIX increases, the price of VXX increases. For example, between February 22nd and March 18th 2020, VXX was up by more than 300% due to the huge spike in volatility caused by COVID-19.

Using an ETN like VXX can be an effective way to hedge against your long-term portfolio and protect your downside during a bear market. You would not want to hold VXX long-term as there is no upside to holding it in a bull market when volatility tends to be low. Like any futures based product, ensure you understand how the instrument works, as well as the risks involved with a product which tracks volatility, because you can lose a significant portion of your investment in a short period of time.

CRYPTOCURRENCY

Cryptocurrencies are the latest sexy asset class that everyone wants to get into. However, this doesn't mean that you automatically should. A majority of attention around this asset class occurred when the price of Bitcoin hit over $19,000 and everyone rushed in to invest in it.

The price now sits at $9,000 and is still subject to extreme volatility. However, the growing acceptance of Bitcoin and other alternative currencies has led to them becoming more mainstream, and as a result they've come to be viewed as safe hedges from fiat currencies.

A fiat currency is paper money. It has no value of its own. For example, the paper that the dollar is printed on is worth nothing. However, it gains value because everyone accepts the use of money as a means to trade goods with one another. Cryptocurrency enthusiasts cite this as an example of how paper money and the currencies attached to it is worthless.

All cryptocurrencies, the good ones at least, seek to achieve a purpose. In the case of Bitcoin, the idea was to create a universal currency that could be used across borders and one that was secure. These aims are now inherent in every cryptocurrency that has been launched. Given that Bitcoin was the first to the scene, these aims were revolutionary when it was first launched.

As an asset class, there is a lot of evidence to suggest that a basket of cryptocurrencies is a great hedge against traditional investments. The long-term evidence of such an investment thesis working out is questionable, though. Many Governments worldwide vehemently oppose cryptos and many have enacted laws that make it impossible to trade with them, even if exchanging them for fiat currencies is allowed.

This has turned crypto into a speculative space, and apart from the initial investors, many currencies attract people hoping to make a quick buck thanks to what they've heard on social media. There is an intelligent way to invest, but this requires the investors to put in some work up front.

For starters, the cryptocurrency's whitepaper is to the currency what the 10-K is to a company. It details everything to do with the currency and, most importantly, the function it is trying to implement. Understanding this process is critical if you're looking to invest in any currency.

This throws up quite a few barriers to the average investor. First there is the technical jargon one needs to understand. Whitepapers are fertile ground for discussion of the technical aspects of blockchain and its enhancements. Some cryptos are even tied to specific platforms and are not meant to be freely traded. For example, there are currencies that are tied to specific computing platforms.

Each coin translates to a certain number of hours that can be used on the computing platform by developers. Such a coin is hardly a good investment for the average investor. The second problematic aspect for the average investor is the culture surrounding the asset class. As things currently stand, no cryptocurrency has utility in our economies.

Even Bitcoin is not traded with any kind of significant volume compared to more traditional financial instruments. This means all currency prices are heavily tied to its price since no one knows which number represents good value. The average market player in this space is a speculator and they're not concerned with the long-term utility aspect of the asset.

The other type of major player in this space is the crypto evangelist who believes that the asset class represents a new paradigm for the world. They may or may not be right in this regard. That's beside the point. The issue is that such people don't care about the money that is present in cryptos. They're investing in something bigger.

The average investor is thus faced with a difficult situation if they aren't an evangelist. A basket of cryptocurrencies might hold some value against the dollar, but it's tough to predict. The evangelists do have a point and cryptocurrencies seem to be here to stay. Even if they don't replace fiat currencies, the online nature of our world means that they'll have some function moving forward.

Given these risks, we recommend investing no more than five percent of your total capital in Bitcoin while leaving the other cryptocurrencies alone unless you are a more experienced investor. The highly speculative nature of Bitcoin will move the value of your portfolio to extremes if it exceeds this limit. Taking a small position is a smart move though, as the potential for 500-1000% gains is still there, and this could prove to be a portfolio-saver if there is a collapse in traditional assets.

PROTECTING YOUR PORTFOLIO & GENERATING EXTRA MONTHLY INCOME WITH RISK-AVERSE OPTIONS STRATEGIES

You might have heard of options if you've dabbled in the markets previously. Options are a derivative instrument and have been called many things in the past. One description that has been applied to them has always been "complicated." This is far from the truth.

Options are a little bit more complex than common stock purchases, but this hardly means you can't understand how they work. What's important for you to grasp is that it isn't the instrument itself that is complex, but the strategy applied that can be complicated.

These instruments lend themselves very well to both simple and highly convoluted strategies. In this chapter, we're going to highlight two simple strategies that you can use to earn steady monthly income. Before we do that though, we have to ask, what are options, and how do they work?

Derivative instruments are identified as such because they derive their value from something else. Options derive their value from what is called the underlying. The underlying could be a stock (it usually is), a bond, an index or a currency pair. Bond options are highly complex and will not be available for you to trade. Most brokers won't offer you currency options either.

This leaves us with stock options, and there are two kinds of them: *calls* and *puts*. *Calls* give you the right but not the obligation to buy the underlying stock at a specified price before a specified date. While *puts* allow you to sell the underlying at a specified price before a specified date.

In plain English: If you own a call, you can choose to buy a stock and if you own a put you can choose to sell it. The price at which you buy or sell is called the strike price and the date before which you can do this is called the expiration date. Like futures, options are also contracts that expire monthly.

Options can be bought and sold in the open market like common stock. The price of an option is called its premium (like an insurance policy). Options pricing is a complicated topic since there are two components to it: the prospects of the underlying and the time left to expiration. To illustrate how complex it is, the professors who developed the model to price options ended up winning the Nobel Prize.

When you buy an option, you cannot earn back the premium. Your profit on the trade is whatever you earn from it minus the option premium.

However, you don't need to understand these intricacies to trade options in simple strategies. What's more important is for you to understand calls and puts and what they signify. You make money on a call when the underlying price increases. With puts, you make money when the underlying price falls.

Here's an example. Let's say you buy a call on Walmart. Below is the relevant information:

Underlying price: $120

Call premium: $10

Call strike price: $130

Call expiry date: One month from purchase date (today)

If the price of Walmart hits or exceeds $130, your call option gives you the right to buy the stock at $130. Let's say it goes up to $145 a week after you buy it. You can now exercise your option and buy Walmart for $130 and sell it back into the market for $145. You've made a profit of $5 per share. (Sale price - Buy price - Call premium = 145-130-10 = 5)

Similarly, here's an example of a put.

Underlying price: $120

Put premium: $10

Put strike price: $110

Put expiry date: One month from purchase date (today)

If the price of Walmart dips below the strike price to say $95, you can sell WMT at $110 (put strike price) and cover your position by buying it back at $95. You've sold at $110 and bought at $95 and this gives you a $5 profit (110-95-10 = 5)

In addition to exercising your option, you can buy and sell the option itself. When the underlying price moves up and down as in the examples above, the option premium moves along with it. This is because the value of the premium changes depending on how close or far away the underlying is from the strike price, as well as the time remaining before the option expires.

If the underlying moves past the call strike price, the call premium is going to rise in value. You can sell the call and collect a profit.

Every options contract covers 100 shares of the underlying. This means you'll need to multiply the option premium by 100 to figure out what you'll have to pay to purchase it. This means options are a leveraged instrument. By purchasing a single option you've gained exposure to 100 shares.

If you don't fully understand your strategy, options can be a dangerous tool. It's a bit like handing the keys to a powerful car to someone who hasn't driven before. In the hands of an experienced driver, the car is capable of performing brilliantly. In the hands of someone who's a poor driver or a novice, it'll end up causing harm to its occupants.

Having said that, the options strategies highlighted here are easy to understand. If you can comprehend sixth grade math, you'll be able to understand how they work. The key to making options work for you is to understand the role time plays.

Options decrease in value drastically when they enter the 30 days before expiration time frame. This means any strategy that you implement needs to run for at least 31 days. If you go long within this timeframe, you're probably not going to capture the fullest extent of the increase in premium prices. This means you're not going to buy any options that are going to expire within a few days. Unless the underlying moves massively, the odds of you making a profit are slim to none.

Let's look at the first options strategy.

PROTECTIVE PUTS

Given that prices will be dropping like flies in a bear market, the first step you can take to secure any long positions is to use protective puts. These will cover your downside risk better than a stop loss order.

A stop loss order is prone to being jumped by the market. In other words, you might set a stop loss order at $35 (after having purchased the stock at $50). If the market experiences huge volatility and if the only prices available in the market are $20 and $25, your broker will sell your order at one of these two prices.

This is despite your stop loss level being defined at $35. It isn't the broker's fault that market prices behaved this way. The stop loss level is just a trigger. It tells your broker to liquidate if the market sinks below that price. It doesn't say that the broker has to execute at the trigger price.

Options give you the ability to fix the price you receive upon exit. If you purchased a put at $35, you now have the right to sell the stock at this price. If the market price dips below this level you can exercise your option and the person who sold you the option has to honor the strike price.

Thus, you sell the underlying for $35. Since you've already bought the stock (for $50), you don't need to cover your position. The protective put isn't a money-making strategy. It's something that ensures your downside is properly protected. Stop loss orders get jumped quite often in bear markets since volatility spikes massively.

The second strategy is a money-making one but requires you to carry out some preliminary prep work.

CASH-SECURED PUTS

Since options can be freely traded in the markets, you can go ahead and sell a put without owning the underlying stock. Selling an option is also referred to as writing one. If you sell/write/short a put, you're betting on the stock price to rise and remain above the put's strike price.

Let's say you see Walmart at $50 and think that it isn't going to dip below $35. You write a put at $35 that expires one month from now. When you write or sell a put, you receive the option premium upfront. This is because the person who bought the put from you pays you this amount.

The option premium also represents your maximum profit from the trade. You might be wondering: If you feel that Walmart won't dip below $35 and will rise, why not buy a call? You could do this. However, the call option is likely going to be expensive. You'll need the stock to rise pretty high in order to clear a profit. Remember, you need to earn the option premium to break even on your trade.

There's no way of predicting how high the stock will rise. If all you know is that the stock won't dip below $35, selling a put is a much simpler way to make money. It removes the pressure of having to predict the degree of the rise. What's more, you earn your profit up front and this is a good way of earning income.

However, since you've sold a put without owning the underlying stock, you're naked. If the price dips below $35, you'll have to deliver the underlying to the buyer. This means you'll have to buy the stock at whatever price it's selling in the market and sell the stock to the option buyer at the strike price.

If Walmart falls to $10, you've just made a loss of $25 per share. On a single options contract that's a loss of $2,500.

Given this risk, many brokers will not allow you to write naked puts. Instead, they will insist on you securing it with either stock or cash. Securing the put with stock means you'll have to buy it and this might not appeal to you. Instead, you can secure it with cash.

The amount of cash you'll need to have on hand to do this is equal to the strike price multiplied by the number of shares you own via the options contract. In our example of Walmart, the strike price is $35 and you own a single option. This means you'll have to have at least $3,500 as cash in your account to cover the maximum potential loss.

The secured put strategy is a great strategy when you think that a stock has hit its lowest point and is now poised to rise higher. Bearish sentiment will be high and put premiums will be overpriced. This means you'll earn a lot more than in normal circumstances. As the put expires, worthless, you get to keep the premium earned.

COMPLEXITY

Options strategies get complicated when you introduce multiple legs into it. Strategies such as vertical spreads use two or even four legs to take advantage of a situation. It's best for you to stay away from them since these strategies require a much deeper understanding of the way options work.

Use puts in a protective fashion or apply the secured put strategy to take advantage of bear markets.

If you'd like a deeper understanding of options, including video examples then we've prepared a free introductory guide called *Options 101* inside our bonus resources section which you can find at:

https://freemanpublications.com/bonus

HOW TO PREPARE FOR THE ABSOLUTE WORST

This chapter is aimed at helping you prepare for an absolute worst-case scenario. We don't believe this is likely to happen anytime soon, but it never hurts to be prepared. In case a crisis does unfold, it's better to have and not need certain items as opposed to not having them and needing them.

STOCKING UP ON ESSENTIAL ITEMS

Supermarkets and grocery stores typically stock two to three days' worth of items in-store. If demand for these essential items runs high, then you're likely going to face empty shelves. It's important to stock up on these items since they run out quickly during times of crisis.

Generators

Backup sources of power are invaluable during tough times. These sell out first. The downside to generators is that they need fuel to run and will make a noise. If this bothers you too much, you can opt for an inverter or even use the battery in your car.

Canned Goods

If you're unlikely to have power, then canned goods are a great source of nutrition. They last long and usually don't need too much cooking to deliver a good meal.

Radios

When the power goes out, you won't have access to the internet or television. Old-fashioned radios will be the only source of communication. Instead of opting for battery-powered radios, buy hand-cranked ones.

Candles

You can stock up on batteries, but they will likely run out at some point. In such situations, candles are great to stock up on. While they don't have to be your primary source of light, they are good backups.

First Aid and Medicine

You'll need to have a first aid box well prepared. Stock it with necessities such as antiseptics, gauze and cotton. You'll also need basic medicine such as paracetamol tablets and ibuprofen. You can opt for generic brands for such medicines since they do the job well.

Make sure you stock up on vitamins too.

Flashlights

Flashlights and headlamps can be your primary light source. Make sure they're solar-powered instead of battery-operated.

Non-Perishable Food and Drinking Water

Stay away from frozen food since you might not have power. Opt for canned food as mentioned previously or food that can be cooked over a grill or a simple stovetop. This will change your purchasing options, so think this through carefully.

Stove

You'll need something to cook your food over. Opt for a propane stove since these are the most practical and safe.

FOOD STORAGE BEST PRACTICES

When it comes to food, storage is extremely important. Start small by storing enough food for three days. Most households will already have enough food for that length of time. Then slowly build up to three weeks and then scale up to three months. Most preppers eventually manage to store enough for a year.

Consider the shelf life of the food you store when buying it. White rice and pasta might not be as healthy as their brown varieties, but they tend to last longer. Foods such as dairy products and vegetable oil will not last long, so it's pointless to store these. Examples of foods that pretty much last forever include:

- Apple cider vinegar
- Cornstarch
- Clarified butter/ghee
- Hard liquor
- Hardtack - made from a mixture of flour and water and is a hard cracker
- Honey
- Salt
- Soy sauce
- Sugar
- White rice

Have a Grab Bag Ready

You never know when an emergency might strike and will force you to leave your home. Having a grab bag of essential items ready at all times is a good idea.

In this, you should have:

- A three-day supply of non-perishable food and a manual can opener
- 2 liters of water per person per day for at least three days
- Phone charger or battery bank
- Hand crank radio
- Hand crank flashlight
- First aid kit
- Extra batteries
- Additional pairs of eyeglasses or contacts
- Copies of important documents along with originals. Passport, certificates, insurance, title deeds etc.
- Garbage bags and moist towelettes
- Seasonal clothing
- Whistle
- Pen and notepad
- Local map

In addition to this you should also have an amount of cash in small bills at home equivalent to your weekly spend. Cash is still king in a worst case scenario, and you will have an easier time bartering with cash than you will precious metals or ammo.

PREPARING FOR THE NEXT TIME—
WHAT TO DO AT THE END OF A BULL MARKET

Make it a point to re-read this book five years from now when the economic outlook is different. People get used to existing conditions pretty quickly and tend to forget that the opposite set of conditions might exist as well. In bear markets we forget that bull markets can exist.

In bull markets, euphoria cons us into thinking that bear markets will never exist. Keep looking out for the signs of overextended markets as we described when talking about the stages of a market. The fact is that bull and bear markets end, and at some point they'll begin as well.

ANTICIPATING CAUSES

As we mentioned earlier, trying to anticipate a single cause for a bear market is futile. Bear markets begin when there are enough reasons built up for the market to fall. All it needs is a catalyst and everything comes tumbling down. Many investors get caught up in trying to find these catalysts.

This is no different from trying to time the market and enter it at an optimal point. Note that all bear markets in the past have been caused by seemingly innocuous things.

1901

This was the first stock market crash that attracted widespread media attention. It began as a soap opera. E.H. Harriman and Jacob Schiff aimed to assume control over the Union Pacific Railroad and were opposed by J.P. Morgan and James Hill. It was a bit like two colossal walls of money clashing against one another.

Given the fact that both sides were trying to gain control of the important railroad, investors piled into railroad stocks and borrowed money heavily to do so. This led to railroad stocks rising to absurd levels. As all smart investors do, Harriman and Schiff (who would win this battle) had amassed their holdings at far lower levels.

Viewing the extremely high valuations, they sold a portion of their holdings without relinquishing control of the company. Word spread that both men were now selling and this caused a colossal crash in railroad stocks that cleaned many market participants out. This precipitated a wave of margin calls that led to sell-offs in every other company listed on the exchange.

Who would have thought a single railroad company could cause such a huge crash? Jesse Livermore, whom we mentioned before, managed to call this crash correctly even though he didn't anticipate that the struggle over Union Pacific would cause it (Lefèvre, 1994).

1906

The cause for this crash was the great earthquake that rocked San Francisco. Initial reports suggested that the fire was contained early on and that there wasn't significant damage. However, as reports kept trickling in, the damage was a lot larger than imagined.

This caused a panic in certain stocks that spread like wildfire to every other stock in the market. You must keep in mind that the telegraph was the only reliable source of communication back then. This made the market extremely susceptible to misinformation.

Jesse Livermore once again managed to call this market. Bizarrely, he did so when vacationing with a friend and wandering into a broker's office. He saw Union Pacific's stock (the railroad was based out of San Francisco) behaving oddly and decided to short it on a hunch (Lefèvre, 1994).

2000

Livermore was long gone by the time the year 2000 rolled around, but the underlying emotions that the market produced were still the same. Internet stocks were all the rage and these were promoted thanks to the advent of online trading. "Online" back then simply meant a real-time feed of prices on broker software, not what we think of today.

The euphoria leading up to the crash was fueled by IPOs from companies who were claiming to eliminate the efficiencies from certain industries, while simultaneously hemorrhaging money themselves. Priceline.com was one of the best examples of this. The company went from $16/share to $88/share on its IPO day, and was valued at $9.8 Billion. At the time this was the largest valuation of a public internet company on its IPO day. This was despite Priceline's core business (allowing consumers to bid on airline tickets at a discount) being a money loser, with no signs of ever becoming profitable. This led to the CEO of rival website CheapTickets famously stating "We've got a policy here at CheapTickets. We need to make money." Many of these overvaluations were caused by Venture Capital firms driving prices up as much as possible, because this is when they got paid. After the initial IPO period, the VC investors would cash out their gigantic profits, and leave retail investors holding the bag.

Perhaps no single statistic was more damning than Mary Meeker's analysis of Internet Stocks in October 1999. Meeker discovered that the market cap of the 199 internet stocks was a whopping $450 billion. But the total annual sales of these companies came to only about $21 billion. And their annual profits? A collective loss of $6.2 Billion.

To paraphrase, Benjamin Graham, the market eventually went from a voting machine to a weighing machine. Company after company declared bankruptcy and the market went into freefall. The Nasdaq peaked at 5,048.62 on March 10th 2000, it would be 15 years before it reached that figure again (McCullough, 2018).

2001

There was a brief bear market towards the end of 2001 that followed 9/11. This was a classic case of an external shock that the average investor could never have foreseen happening.

2008

This one was building up for years, if not decades. Everyone forgot that home prices could go down as well as up. Lending standards collapsed. Strawberry pickers were given money to buy million-dollar homes. The ratings agencies abdicated responsibility and a few Wall Street banks managed to get out of the burning house before locking the door behind them.

2020

This one was also a decade in the making. Cheap money caused high levels of leverage and papered over cracks in the economy. Everyone knew the party would come to an end at some point. It eventually did when a bat infected a pangolin that ended up being eaten by someone in Wuhan, China.

The virus spread and the fragile market came crashing down. No one could have foreseen that a virus would bring things down before it occurred. There have been a few investors who acted swiftly once they heard of the virus.

Bill Ackman from the previous Herbalife story is one of them. He was one of the first American voices to warn against the lackadaisical attitude of the American government and he was proven right. Some sources estimate Ackman has cleared over a billion dollars acting on his convictions (Winck, 2020).

LESSONS

The point of this history lesson is to show that there is no limit to the number of things that can prompt a bear market. In the five stages of the economic cycle that we referenced earlier in this book, you must remember that it doesn't matter *what* the shock is. All that matters is that there is one. And the underlying causes of all shocks are the same. Euphoria and complacency are present throughout. While many think the markets have become even more unstable these days, the fact is that the early 1900s were far more unstable.

This was due to the lack of regulation. The formation of the SEC led to an era of relatively stable markets before technology introduced the lack of regulation right back. Will we see an era of better regulation governing technology? Or will instability continue?

There's no point trying to predict this. All the investor can do is look for the telltale signs and act accordingly. We previously mentioned the death cross technical indicator in chapter 6. This is one of the tools you can use to be prepared for a potential crash. Do not be hesitant to move your holdings into cash if you spot the signs of an overvalued market. Remember that holding cash is a position in itself. This is especially true if you are closer to, or currently in retirement.

HOW TO IDENTIFY FRAUDULENT OPERATIONS

The start of bear markets typically brings to light a variety of fraudulent behavior. Many companies that were coasting along during the good times get exposed and an almighty ruckus ensues. The popular media comes up with quotes about how the signs were there for everyone to see.

They carefully sidestep the fact that they were amongst those that missed the signs. Despite all of this, there are a few telling markers that reveal instances of fraudulent activity.

SMARTER THAN EVERYONE ELSE

Appearing to be smarter than everyone else is a tried and tested con artist strategy. Our brains are extremely susceptible to appearances and as long as something looks right, we ignore other rational evidence. Someone wearing a fancy suit must be wealthy while the guy riding the bus must be poor.

This bias triggers our confirmation bias and with the blinders firmly on we grow hostile towards information that contradicts our opinion. The "too smart for common folk" technique has been used by financial frauds repeatedly.

Enron and its incomparable CEO Jeff Skilling were famous for this attitude (McLean & Elkind, 2004). Skilling famously created an atmosphere of intellectual intimidation at Enron and repeatedly used words like smart and complex to describe Enron's strategies. At the end of the day, all he was doing was making things up as he went along.

Another example was Bernie Madoff (Arvedlund, 2008). Madoff used a childishly simple options strategy to supposedly earn 15% returns every year like clockwork. Veteran options traders, even retail ones, wondered how that strategy could earn such astronomical returns. Madoff's constant refrain was that his methods were more sophisticated and that others didn't understand his genius.

Complexity by itself isn't a problem, but it is a red flag when the creator of the complexity cannot seemingly explain it in detail. This was amply evident with Madoff. Add to the fact that everyone was raving about him, and you have a scenario that screams fraudulent activity.

NOTHING CAN GO WRONG

Another key component of fraudulent investment opportunities is that they have an air of nothing possibly going wrong. Real investment opportunities always have risks attached to them. Smart investors understand that risk needs to be correlated to reward in order to justify an investment decision. Anyone who claims you can make 20% per month or 200% per year, every year, is either outright lying or is not explaining the huge amount of risk involved in such a strategy.

While every investment opportunity carries risk, assuming this risk is justified if the reward on offer is large. If you don't have money for college, you could assume student loan debt. This might be a good decision if you can find a high-paying job after school. It's a terrible decision if you decide to study art history.

Every investor's risk appetite is different and this is why there's no such thing as a can't-miss opportunity. If you don't have the mindset to handle the risk inherent in an opportunity, you will screw it up. Most investors don't want this to happen. They want to be comfortable at all times and want money to flow in easily. They don't want to work for it.

Frauds latch onto this and exploit it at every turn. What's more, they charge exorbitant amounts of money or nothing at all for this "system." Skilling charged his investors huge amounts through stock options and dumped his stock when he saw the writing on the wall. Madoff famously never charged anything for his money management services.

The zero-fee ploy is seemingly a polar opposite to the high-fee ploy, but both have the same psychological effect. They lead you to believe you've found a gold mine and confirmation bias kicks in.

Internet companies that went bust in the dotcom crash employed similar tactics. By being technology companies, they couldn't fail (at least that's what they said). They used stock options to reward their executives since they didn't have enough cash to do so. They used their stock prices to borrow heavily from banks who had a history of lending to exactly the kind of people who shouldn't be given money.

The presence of buzzwords cause FOMO to manifest and the next thing you know people have placed their life savings into such companies. The use of sophisticated phrases and words by themselves are signs of fraud. This perpetuates the theme that the investor or person in charge of the opportunity is a genius.

LUCK VERSUS COMPETENCE

Every so often an incompetent person manages to make tons of money. Even broken clocks are right twice a day. Spotting whether money was made due to sheer luck or due to competence is a tough task. Keep in mind that even the best investments need some luck in order to work out.

The proportion of luck versus skill is what you want to look at. In every investment opportunity, you want to be siding with skill as much as possible since this is a more repeatable process. Relying on luck is a bit like investing your money in lottery tickets and hoping that they'll pay out someday.

A great way to spot whether an investment manager is relying on skill is to look at their circle of competence and match that to the investment opportunity. If Steve Jobs came up to you and told you to invest in Apple back in 2004, you would have done well to follow that advice.

If he came up to you and told you to invest in the Segway, that would have been a dumb decision. Even Steve Jobs was subject to the circle of competence. Jobs was one of the investors who famously placed money in the Segway along with a number of other luminaries. The company was founded by a famous inventor who had a brilliant track record.

The only issue was that every single one of them were well outside their circle of competence. The inventor hailed from a medical device background and there wasn't a single person from anything remotely resembling transportation devices on board. In hindsight, the Segway might be thought of as being ahead of its time.

However, people who understand their circle of competence usually manage to time their products right. We're not suggesting in any way that the Segway is an example of fraud. It's just that even great opportunities backed by highly trustworthy people can end up relying on luck instead of skill.

In the annals of corporate fraud in America, Elizabeth Holmes comes a close second to Skilling purely because her company Theranos was a private operation. If it was public, there's no doubt she would have surpassed him easily.

Holmes checked all the right boxes of fraud. She was intelligent sounding, had the right pedigree (Stanford dropout which in the entrepreneurial world is immediately equated to genius), a complex solution to a complex problem, used heavy-sounding terms and ran a company that practiced absurd levels of secrecy.

She had the right people around her too. Former statesmen, U.S. Armed Forces generals and former CEOs littered her board of directors. She was pals with Chelsea Clinton, which meant Hillary was close by. Henry Kissinger was involved too, which satisfied the Republican crowd (Carreyrou, 2011).

Everything was perfect! Except it wasn't. Holmes had zero competence in the medical field. She was a chemical engineering major and dropped out after freshman year. She played the technology disruption card. Her patent was all she leaned on, but that was just a piece of paper. Investors forget that a patent without a working prototype is useless.

When it came crashing down, there was disbelief followed by "we knew it all along" reporting. Holmes is trying to raise money for her next company despite facing the prospect of spending the rest of her life in jail. Given her skill set, she might even succeed.

Con artists use charisma and the previous two points to obscure the fact that everything depends on getting lucky. Holmes started off as an idealist teenager trying to do good but somewhere along the way her inner con artist asserted itself. She never had competence to begin with and began relying on luck. Naturally, this doesn't work over and over as a strategy.

She got lucky a few times and resorted to fraud moving forward when she couldn't replicate it.

ALWAYS HAS AN ANSWER

The smartest of people understand that there are many things they don't know. The dumbest among us are fully convinced that they know everything. What's more, they're so sure of it that they end up convincing the intelligent ones too. Life can be ironic like that.

Be very careful of an investment adviser or principal who seems to know the answer to everything or has an inability to say "I don't know." You obviously don't want someone who says this all the time. This merely indicates that they're well outside their circle of competence.

However, a field such as investing has so many variables that it is impossible for someone to know everything. Ask Warren Buffett about the global economy and the first thing he says is that he doesn't know. Ask George Soros about the prospects of a particular company and he responds by saying he doesn't know.

Intelligent investors know what they don't know. By avoiding a reliance on such matters they ensure the odds are on their side. It's only the unknowns they need to worry about.

How to Adopt this Process in the Next 18-24 Months

If there was an apt slogan for bear markets, it would be: Keep Calm and Carry On. Our emotional biases make it seem as if bear markets and bad times will persist forever, but this is just an illusion. The truth is that everything ends, even bear markets.

Capitalizing on bear markets requires a different skill set from the ones that allow you to thrive in bullish conditions. In bear markets, there is no place to hide, and it will seem as if everything is close to collapse. The place to begin is to evaluate the stage the bear market is in.

Different stages call for different strategies and we've highlighted a number of these. For example, the cash-protected put option is a great strategy for phase five of the economic cycle. The biggest challenge you will face will be presented by your own mindset. We're naturally conditioned to value the good times and be extremely fearful of the bad.

This causes us to shun bear markets and sit them out. However, intelligent investors realize that bear markets are the ones that provide huge entry opportunities in great companies. Investors overreact to bad news, and as a result everything gets sold. This means perfectly good companies with strong businesses end up being priced at bargain levels.

Transforming the way you view bear markets is crucial to your success. Uncertainty equals opportunity in such times. The media and social media will push the narrative that markets will never recover from the current crisis. Every little rally in the market will be celebrated joyously.

People will rush into the markets, believing in them, and will promptly get burned. As an intelligent investor, your job is to remain as rational as possible, and the best way to do this is to examine the layers related to the company from the inside out. The best place to begin is the 10-K, and we've broken down how you need to go about looking at the important points in this filing.

Company press releases and earnings calls contain factual information, but this is often wrapped in a heavy degree of spin. Social media and your neighbor are the last places you should think of when it comes to collecting information. Tweet-happy CEOs and press departments manipulate perception of companies and you should stay away from this as much as possible.

We carry a large number of biases within us, and these cloud our judgment. We've highlighted the most important ones in this book. While it might be close to impossible to get rid of all of them, it pays to remain aware of them. By bringing awareness, you'll be able to avoid some of the huge problems that these biases create.

Avoid traps such as forming narratives tied to investment and looking for quick riches. This will cause you to jump into poor investments that will cost you money. Before jumping into the market make sure you have a healthy amount of cash in the bank. Invest only the money that you can afford to lose.

Gold and silver are examples of asset classes that do well in turbulent times. In this age of quantitative easing and money printing, the case for these assets gets better by the day. You could short the industries that perform poorly. Airlines and hospitality companies tend to be hit the hardest during tough times. Their business economics are poor and there are telltale signs to spot such companies.

You could also invest in sector-specific ETFs to hedge your investments against a declining market. Lastly, cryptocurrencies are also a good hedge, but these bring their own risks to the table. You can also use options strategies to protect your investments as well as bring additional income every month.

While the worst-case scenario might be far away, it helps to be prepared. We've provided you with brief guidelines on how you can go about doing this. Stop looking for reasons the market might fail and instead learn what you need to do. Spot fraudulent activity before you fall for it and you'll do just fine.

Bear markets are tough, but with the right process and mindset, you will get through them and thrive. We wish you the best of luck with your investments and hope you've learned to view bear markets differently thanks to reading this book!

"THE MOST SUCCESSFUL PEOPLE IN LIFE ARE THE ONES WHO ASK QUESTIONS. THEY'RE ALWAYS LEARNING. THEY'RE ALWAYS GROWING. THEY'RE ALWAYS PUSHING."

- Robert Kiyosaki

REFERENCES

Arvedlund, E. (2008). What We Wrote About Madoff. Retrieved 29 May 2020, from https://www.barrons.com/articles/SB122973813073623485?tesla=y

Banton, C. (2020). Trading the Gold-Silver Ratio. Retrieved 29 May 2020, from https://www.investopedia.com/articles/trading/09/gold-silver-ration.asp

Beattie, A. (2019). Silver Thursday: How Two Wealthy Traders Cornered The Market. Retrieved 29 May 2020, from https://www.investopedia.com/articles/optioninvestor/09/silver-thursday-hunt-brothers.asp

Bernstein, R. (2018). Retrieved 29 May 2020, from https://www.rbadvisors.com/images/pdfs/toward_the_sounds_of_chaos.pdf

Brook, D. (2016). How Dubai Became Dubai. Retrieved 29 May 2020, from https://nextcity.org/daily/entry/how-dubai-became-dubai

Burry, M. (2010). I Saw the Crisis Coming. Why Didn't the Fed? Retrieved 17 June 2020, from https://www.nytimes.com/2010/04/04/opinion/04burry.html

Carreyrou, J. Bad blood.

Chamaria, N. (2018). Why This Struggling Silver Stock Rocketed 51% in November | The Motley Fool. Retrieved 29 May 2020, from https://www.fool.com/investing/2018/12/05/why-this-struggling-silver-stock-rocketed-51-in-no.aspx

Chen, J. (2020). Understanding Treasury Notes. Retrieved 29 May 2020, from https://www.investopedia.com/terms/t/treasurynote.asp

Chen, J. (2019). Sir John Templeton. Retrieved 29 May 2020, from https://www.investopedia.com/terms/s/sirjohntempleton.asp

Cheng, E. (2017). $24 million iced tea company says it's pivoting to the blockchain, and its stock jumps 200%. Retrieved 29 May 2020, from https://www.cnbc.com/2017/12/21/long-island-iced-tea-micro-cap-adds-blockchain-to-name-and-stock-soars.html

Colarusso, D. (2020). Mirror Mirror on the Wall, Explain for Me a Put and Call. Retrieved 29 May 2020, from https://www.thestreet.com/investing/options/mirror-mirror-on-the-wall-explain-for-me-a-put-and-call-964257

Dastin, J., & Saleem, N. (2015). Dubai airline Emirates rejects Delta apology over 9/11 comments. Retrieved 13 June 2020, from https://www.reuters.com/article/us-emirates-airlines-delta/dubai-airline-emirates-rejects-delta-apology-over-9-11-comments-idUSKBN0LN1S320150219

Delinquency Rate on Credit Card Loans, All Commercial Banks. (2020). Retrieved 29 May 2020, from https://fred.stlouisfed.org/series/DRCCLACBS

Emspak, J. (2020). Why Is the Price of Gold More Than Just Supply and Demand?. Retrieved 29 May 2020, from https://www.investopedia.com/articles/active-trading/031915/what-moves-gold-prices.asp

Floyd, D. (2019). Buffett's Bet with the Hedge Funds: And the Winner Is …. Retrieved 29 May 2020, from https://www.investopedia.com/articles/investing/030916/buffetts-bet-hedge-funds-year-eight-brka-brkb.asp

Garret, O. (2017). 3 Reasons Why Investors Should Avoid Gold ETFs. Retrieved 29 May 2020, from https://www.forbes.com/sites/oliviergarret/2017/03/09/3-reasons-why-investors-should-avoid-gold-etfs/#2c535f754dd8

Green, T. (2016). This Warren Buffett Quote Describes Twitter Perfectly | The Motley Fool. Retrieved 29 May 2020, from https://www.fool.com/investing/2016/11/30/this-warren-buffett-quote-describes-twitter-perfec.aspx

Guide to Analyst Recommendations. (2020). Retrieved 29 May 2020, from https://www.marketwatch.com/tools/guide.asp

Han, W. (2020). Investors Sip the Bitter Taste of the Luckin Coffee Scandal.

Retrieved 19 June 2020, from https://www.caixinglobal.com/2020-04-20/in-depth-investors-sip-the-bitter-taste-of-the-luckin-coffee-scandal-101544557.html

Hayes, A. (2019). History of the Dutch Tulip Bulb Market's Bubble. Retrieved 29 May 2020, from https://www.investopedia.com/terms/d/dutch_tulip_bulb_market_bubble.asp

Heaton, C. (2016). Retrieved 29 May 2020, from https://moneyweek.com/430541/bill-gross-is-still-bearish

Iacurci, G. (2020). Unemployment is nearing Great Depression levels. Here's how the eras are similar — and different. Retrieved 29 May 2020, from https://www.cnbc.com/2020/05/19/unemployment-today-vs-the-great-depression-how-do-the-eras-compare.html

Kagan, J. (2020). Maintenance Margin Definition. Retrieved 29 May 2020, from https://www.investopedia.com/terms/m/maintenancemargin.asp

Kettleman, J., & Schultz, K. (2020). Modi Orders 3-Week Total Lockdown for All 1.3 Billion Indians. Retrieved 29 May 2020, from https://www.nytimes.com/2020/03/24/world/asia/india-coronavirus-lockdown.html

Koster, J. (2018). Jim Chanos on primary research and peeling the onion… Retrieved 29 May 2020, from https://www.valueinvestingworld.com/2018/04/jim-chanos-on-primary-research-and.html

Lefèvre, E. (1994). Reminiscences of a stock operator. New York: Wiley.

Lewis, M. (2008). The Big Short.

Logan, B. (2020). The world's 20 best airlines for 2019. Retrieved 29 May 2020, from https://www.businessinsider.com/best-airlines-in-the-world-2019-skytrax-rankings-2019-6

Marte, J. (2020). U.S. household debt tops $14 trillion and reaches new record. Retrieved 29 May 2020, from https://www.reuters.com/article/us-usa-fed-household-debt/u-s-household-debt-tops-14-trillion-and-reaches-new-record-idUSKBN20521Z

McLean, B., & Elkind, P. (2004). The smartest guys in the room. London:

Penguin.

McCullough, B. (2018). An eye-opening look at the dot-com bubble of the 2000 – and how it shapes our lives today. Retrieved 18 June 2020, from https://ideas.ted.com/an-eye-opening-look-at-the-dot-com-bubble-of-2000-and-how-it-shapes-our-lives-today/

Mercer, C. (2020). EBITDA's "Naughty 11" Problems and What to Do About Them. Retrieved 29 May 2020, from https://chrismercer.net/ebitdas-naughty-11-problems-and-what-to-do-about-them/

Monica, P. (2018). Bill Ackman's Herbalife disaster is finally over. Retrieved 29 May 2020, from https://money.cnn.com/2018/03/01/investing/herbalife-bill-ackman-carl-icahn/index.html

O'Brien, M. (2012). John Maynard Keynes Was the Warren Buffett of His Day. Retrieved 29 May 2020, from https://www.theatlantic.com/business/archive/2012/04/john-maynard-keynes-was-the-warren-buffett-of-his-day/255356/

Parrish, S. (2020). How Darwin Thought: The Golden Rule of Thinking. Retrieved 29 May 2020, from https://fs.blog/2016/01/charles-darwin-thinker/

Ponzio, J. (2007). Enron: Accounting Scandal or Bad Business | Joe Ponzio's F Wall Street. Retrieved 29 May 2020, from https://www.fwallstreet.com/article/54-enron-accounting-scandal-or-bad-business

Schroeder, A. (2008). The snowball. London: Bloomsbury.

SEC.gov | Facebook to Pay $100 Million for Misleading Investors About the Risks It Faced From Misuse of User Data. (2019). Retrieved 29 May 2020, from https://www.sec.gov/news/press-release/2019-140

Segal, T. (2020). Enron Scandal: The Fall of a Wall Street Darling. Retrieved 29 May 2020, from https://www.investopedia.com/updates/enron-scandal-summary/

Summers, J. (2020). Bloomberg. Retrieved 29 May 2020, from https://www.bloomberg.com/news/articles/2020-03-30/oil-etf-seen-as-tourist-trap-with-crude-trading-in-the-20s

Tesla Q1 2020 Vehicle Production & Deliveries. (2020). Retrieved 29 May

2020, from https://ir.tesla.com/news-releases/news-release-details/tesla-q1-2020-vehicle-production-deliveries

Tesla. (2020). 10-K. New York: Tesla Inc.

The Voting and Weighing Machines. (2020). Retrieved 29 May 2020, from https://news.morningstar.com/classroom2/course.asp?docId=142901&page=7

Tuovila, A. (2020). Generally Accepted Accounting Principles (GAAP). Retrieved 29 May 2020, from https://www.investopedia.com/terms/g/gaap.asp

When Did Concorde First Fly to North America?. (2020). Retrieved 29 May 2020, from https://www.historyhit.com/concorde-opens-london-new-york-route/

Who Benefits From Loaning Shares in a Short Sale?. (2020). Retrieved 29 May 2020, from https://www.investopedia.com/ask/answers/05/shortsalebenefit.asp

Winck, B. (2020). Billionaire investor Bill Ackman turned $27 million into $2.6 billion by betting that the coronavirus would tank the market | Markets Insider. Retrieved 29 May 2020, from https://markets.businessinsider.com/news/stocks/bill-ackman-hedge-profits-billions-coronavirus-tanks-stock-market-economy-2020-3-1029035562

Winck, B. (2020). Gold prices will nearly double to a record $3,000 as central banks fuel 'financial repression,' Bank of America says | Markets Insider. Retrieved 29 May 2020, from https://markets.businessinsider.com/news/stocks/gold-price-target-record-central-bank-stimulus-bank-america-double-2020-4-1029113912